Books

FICTION

The Wishing Rock series
(novels with recipes)
Letters from Wishing Rock
The Wishing Rock Theory of Life
The Tides of Wishing Rock

NONFICTION

The Pam on the Map travel series
(wit and wanderlust)
Iceland
Retrospective: Switzerland
Retrospective: Ireland

From the Wishing Rock Kitchens: Recipes from the Series

~

www.pamstucky.com
twitter.com/pamstucky
facebook.com/pamstuckyauthor
pinterest.com/pamstucky

Pam on the Map
ICELAND

Wit & Wanderlust
Pam Stucky

This is more or less a work of nonfiction, with a nod to the fact that the author has a bad memory and may have gotten some things wrong. Nonetheless, some names may have been changed to protect the innocent and/or the guilty.

Published in the United States by Wishing Rock Press.

Cover photos and design by Pam Stucky
Author photo by Haley Christine Photography

ISBN: 1940800005
ISBN-13: 978-1-940800-00-4
eBook ISBN-13: 978-1-940800-01-1
eBook ISBN: 1940800013

www.wishingrockpress.com

for those who wander and those who wonder

Contents

continued

Contents, continued

Chapter Page

Pam on the Map

What is Pam on the Map?

Simple! The Pam on the Map books are the stories of my adventures around the world, told more or less in real time. As of October 2013, there are three Pam on the Map books: Iceland, Ireland, and Switzerland. The Ireland and Switzerland books are what I call the "retrospective" series, books based on trips I took before the idea for this series was born, and are therefore much shorter. This book, *Pam on the Map: Iceland*, is the first book written specifically for a wider audience. Future Pam on the Map books will cover countries, regions, cities, or even experiences.

Who is Pam?

Pam is me, Pam Stucky. I'm an author, traveler, backseat philosopher, and a person who is intensely curious about people and the world. I've written a series of fiction books — the Wishing Rock series — and am now excited to combine my loves of writing and travel in this new travelogue series: Pam on the Map.

Unbeknownst to me at the time, the seed for the Pam on the Map books was planted in 2005, when I went on my first solo trip to Ireland. I wanted to find a way to stay connected with home, so I researched the location of internet cafés (remember those?) throughout the country. They were common enough, even if sometimes I had to walk a mile or two to get to them. I'd sit down, log in, check the computer for any nefarious "save password" settings that would leave my personal information on the public computer, and write. On these foreign keyboards, slightly different with random keys transposed, I sent home the tales of my travels as a way of bringing others along on my adventures, even if I was technically traveling alone.

I soon heard that people were enjoying my trip reports so much that they were forwarding the emails to friends, who enjoyed them as well. People I didn't even know were sending requests through mutual friends to be added to my email list. Sending home my little missives of my travels truly enhanced my experience. For me, as a storyteller and writer, the joy of travel lies not just in the experience but also in sharing it with others and re-living it through the re-telling.

I've always wanted to write books of immersive travel — tales of my adventures and misadventures as I become familiar with a country or region, taking the readers along on the trip. But gathering enough tales to fill a full book would mean staying in a country for longer, frankly, than I could afford. With the advent of ebooks, however, the world of publishing has opened up. And so I went back to the emails I'd sent from Ireland (2005) and Switzerland (2007) to see how much revising they'd need to mold them to the format I envisioned for the Pam on the Map series. On re-reading them I decided I really liked them in their original format. I saw immediately that they would lose their original flavor and flow if

I changed them. To maintain the integrity of these messages in their raw, shiny innocence, I decided to leave them more or less as is. Those emails are now *Pam on the Map: Ireland* and *Pam on the Map: Switzerland*.

At the same time, I knew I wanted to take a trip — at least one! — specifically for the purpose of writing up my experiences for a new Pam on the Map book. This book, *Pam on the Map: Iceland*, is the first of these. I am hopeful there will be many more to come.

Be sure to come find me online and let me know where you think I should go next! Find me at www.pamstucky.com.

Itinerary

July 30 through August 11, 2013

- July 30: Arrived Keflavík airport
- July 30: Reykjavík; accommodations: friend's house
- July 31: Vík; accommodations: Hotel Lundi
- August 1: Hali; accommodations: Hali Country Hotel
- August 2–4: Akureyri; accommodations: Sæluhús Akureyri
- August 5–6: Hellissandur; accommodations: Hotel Hellissandur
- August 7–10: Reykjavík; accommodations: friend's house
- August 11: Departed Keflavík airport

Map © Pam Stucky; not to scale

Departure

Monday, July 29, 2013

4 a.m.

I'm awake. I'm awake, and I'm going to die.

No, really. I'm about to head to the airport, and I hate flying. I get anxious before I fly. Mildly anxious for a week or so, intensely anxious the day or two before take-off. A couple hours before take-off, I'm sure I'm about to meet my doom.

But, doom or no doom, I'm going anyway. Today, I meet Iceland.

It's nothing new for people to ask why I've chosen to visit any particular country; it's a natural question, after all. Of all the countries in the world, what made you pick this one? Is it something I'm missing out on? What's the draw? What are you going to do there? Should I go too? But with Iceland, there's a bit more incredulity behind the question.

"Why *Iceland*?" I can hear the italics in their voices.

Why Iceland? As with any country, my first thought is, why not? There are so many places I want to go in the world. I love travel, I love seeing new places and meeting new people. But why Iceland, specifically? For me, the answer goes back more than a decade. Fifteen or twenty years ago, my book group read Pico Iyer's *Falling Off the Map: Some Lonely Places of the World*. In it, Iyer reflects on his experiences in a variety of places that are in some way isolated, whether geographically, politically, or otherwise. One of the countries he wrote about was Iceland. Before reading the book I had little knowledge about or interest in Iceland, but after reading Iyer's lyrical prose — he's one of the best travel writers out there — my interest was piqued. What was this magical place he'd visited? I knew that one day, I would go.

More recently, it seems Iceland has become the "it" destination. Possibly because of dirt-cheap winter airfares direct from Seattle to Keflavík, suddenly everyone is going to Iceland, or knows someone who has gone to Iceland, or is thinking about going to Iceland. To top it off, a woman I once worked with now lives in Reykjavík, and she posted an open invitation to anyone who might want to visit, offering up her house as a place to stay.

Thus, Iceland has been on my radar for a while. I was sure I'd make it there in 2012 — so sure, in fact, that I wrote the country into my second Wishing Rock novel, thinking I'd have time to visit and research before writing book three. That didn't happen, so in the third book Iceland became Hawaii. (Naturally.) But in my own life, for my own purposes, I still wanted to go and see this mystical place.

And so, one day, I made the decision to go.

"I'm going to Iceland!" I texted a friend.

"Can I come along?" she texted back.

So for a short time, I had a travel partner, but as so often happens, that fell through. No worries, I've traveled solo before. I had to adjust my plans a bit, as traveling solo is more expensive than traveling with someone else — splitting the car rental, gas, and hotel costs makes a huge difference — but I still wanted to go.

And that leads us to today, now, 4 a.m. on July 29, 2013, a Monday. I haven't slept well, which is inconvenient as I don't sleep well on planes and my flight lands in Keflavík at 6:45 a.m. Iceland time. (Despite often being called the Reykjavík airport, the international airport is in Keflavík, not Reykjavík; it's about a forty-five-minute drive away.) I have a very full first day planned, so whatever sleep I got last night is all I'll get for a while.

My flight is late in the day — 4:30 p.m. or so — so I don't need to be up early, but I know I'm done sleeping for the night. A million thoughts are flipping through my head like an out-of-control Rolodex. (Remember those?!) I've printed off my eleven-page itinerary, but I don't feel nearly well-enough prepared. Normally, I plan for a year, but this trip came up a little unexpectedly, relatively speaking, and I've only had a few months to plan. I feel rushed. I'm sure I've overlooked important information. I know I will find I should have taken a better or different route around the country, should have stayed in a different town or hotel, should have visited a different place. I can't go yet. I need more time.

But today's the day. Ready or not, it's time to go.

And so I go. The flight is just under seven hours long, and Iceland is about seven hours ahead of Seattle. That means that on the flight over I lose a day, and coming back I'll land just shortly after I leave (the flight is slightly longer coming west than going east).

Six and a half hours into the flight, I have not slept a wink. The flight is miserable. I am fidgety and not a good flyer. I get the full-body equivalent of restless leg syndrome when I fly long distances, twitching and turning and getting up to go to the bathroom just so I can get out of my seat (which is why I always ask for aisle, even though window is so much better), and in general undoubtedly making my seatmates wish for someone else to sit next to.

Then, with thirty minutes to go on the flight, I fall asleep, hard.

It's too late. There's no time to sleep. Put your seat backs up, we're about to land.

It is Tuesday, July 30, 6:45 a.m., and my day is just beginning.

Arrival and
The Golden Circle

Tuesday, July 30, 2013

It's not often that within four hours of arriving in a foreign country I find myself in a swimsuit with a stranger rubbing her hands all over me, in public. And yet, having done that today, I highly recommend it.

It was at Blue Lagoon, of course — Iceland's famous geothermal spa, that is, not the 80s movie — where I indulged in an in-water massage as soon as I could get there from the airport.

But we are getting ahead of ourselves. Let's go back to the beginning of the day.

We left off, of course, without any official nighttime or real sleep to mark the transition from yesterday to today. Monday has blurred into Tuesday, Seattle has blurred into Keflavík. Day has blurred back into day; although the plane chased the sunset on the way over, the sunset slipped south of the plane and merged back into sunrise instead. I'm surprisingly alert, but then it's really only just after midnight at home. A late night, but not unheard of. The real test will come as the day wears on.

The plane has landed, and I did not die. I consider this a very good beginning to the trip.

Now. Before we get on with the rest of the story, let's pause for a moment, shall we, to admire the restrooms at Keflavík International Airport.

Because, of course, the first thing one does on exiting a plane, or the first thing I do anyway, is find a restroom. And here, in Keflavík … people, I don't know if all the restrooms are like this, but the ones I found are the most spacious, luxurious airport bathrooms I've ever seen. They're enormous. By which I mean, the individual stalls are huge. Huge! Each room — because they're not really stalls; no, these are individual rooms — has a toilet AND its own sink. All in the one big room! If I were to guess, which I am doing now, I'd say the rooms are … well, at least 4' by 6'. Each room! After seven hours crunched into my airplane seat — even if Icelandair does have rather good legroom — the space, this little toilet space, all mine (for a couple minutes, anyway), feels scandalously extravagant. Like it was supposed to be saved for someone else, someone famous, someone with an entourage, maybe. But no, the whole room is here just for me! And for everyone else before and after me, but not at the same time, because that would be weird. I have the fleeting, flight-weary idea that I could set up a cot inside the room and take a little nap. But there is much to be done today, and I must be off!

Note, though, when you fly into Keflavík: Don't miss the toilets. They are a sanctuary of peace and joy within a chaotic place. You may not want to leave.

Oh: I need to tell you one more thing about the toilets. The Icelandic word for "toilet" or "restroom" is snyrting. No, I'm not even kidding you. That's a real word. You'll see "WC" (water closet) much more frequently, but you'll also see snyrting. That's the bathroom. I don't know the literal translation. It sounds more like something you'd do in the bathroom than the bathroom itself, like maybe it's a word for that thing when you're in a public restroom and you can't go because all you can do is think about the fact that people are listening and that keeps you from being able to pee, and you end up taking ten times longer than normal and you just know everyone is going to think, "Dang, she was in there a really long time, what the heck was she doing in there?," that could be snyrting, but no, it's the restroom itself. There you go. Snyrting.

Post-flight visit to the snyrting: Done. Iceland is already quite exciting. What next?

Well, this is one thing that in my groggy jet lag fog, I completely forgot about. I'm told that at the airport, liquor is forty to sixty percent cheaper than anywhere else on the island. If a person plans to imbibe, then the time to buy is in the duty-free shops on the way out of Keflavík. I forget, though, so it's an irrelevant point for me, but when you fly in, if you like a little hair of the dog, a little pick-me-up, a little evening tonic, it's something to consider.

Moving on then. One thing I'd been excited for on my trip was the fact that Route 1, my car rental company, had told me they'd have someone at the airport waiting for me with my name on a placard, to take me to the rental place. Awesome! I am so special! My name on a placard! (I know, I'm easily impressed.) I weave and wind my way through the somewhat confusing airport, generally following the other passengers and hoping we'll all eventually end up at the right place. Finally, we walk through a door and ... there they are! Ten or fifteen people, mostly men, looking excruciatingly bored, holding up signs with people's names on them.

So it's not just me, then. I'm not all that special after all.

Especially since none of the signs has my name on it.

I look again.

Nope, still no "Pam Stucky."

Try as I might, I cannot make my name appear on a sign simply by using the Power Of My Mind. (I try this often, actually, try to make things happen simply by using the Power Of My Mind. It never works, but I persist.)

Where are they? Where's my rental company? Where's my guy? How do I get a hold of them? I can't call as I don't have a local phone yet, and it hadn't occurred to me to bring their phone number anyway. I brought my iPhone along with me, but have all cellular data turned off because I don't want to accidentally have my phone start roaming and run up a thousand-dollar phone bill. But I should be able to email them, right? Would they even be checking email at 7:15 a.m.? I'd told them to pick me up at 8, but I said it with the caveat that my flight was coming in at 6:45, and if they had a better idea of what time I'd be emptying out into the pick-up zone, they should use their judgment over mine. Were they just planning to come at 8? Holding my phone out in front of me, I drift through the Placard Zone until my phone gets the slightest WiFi signal. I send an email to Route 1, Whatsapp my parents to let them know I've arrived safely, and wait.

I wander the small area where the men with the placards are and watch, green with envy, as one by one they pair up with their placard-mates. I go to the nearby ATM and withdraw money, chatting with other travelers about the fact that one machine has no cash in it, while my mind fuzzes as I try to figure out whether I want to withdraw 40,000 ISK or 80,000 ISK. The huge numbers confuse me until I remember I've printed out a currency conversion chart. 40,000 ISK (Icelandic krona) is around $340. That should get me through for a while. I go to an airport store and buy an Iceland map and a north Iceland map. And I wait.

I roam the room some more, waving my phone around, trying to get a signal. I check to see whether the car rental company has returned my email.

And I wait.

And finally, I see a young man coming through the door, looking rushed, a placard in hand. Is that my name on it? … YES! My Route 1 knight in shining armor. He has arrived.

He is a lovely young man, dark haired and bright eyed, but when he tells me his name I am still flushed with the excitement that he's arrived at all, and it doesn't register in my brain. I can't guess his age, either, other than "young." I'm not good at guessing ages anymore. I always assume everyone is about my age, but I keep getting younger (don't you?), so it's hard to tell. People my age look so old! I don't look that old, surely. Neither does he. He just finished his first year in law school, that's about all I know.

When he drives me from the Placard Zone to the Route 1 office, Car Rental Guy (as I shall now call him) explains that "We don't have an office, really. We have a WAN."

Really? They have a wide area network? I am confused.

"You have a what?"

"A WAN."

"………"

And then, it dawns on me. A VAN. V for van, pronounced like a W by some Icelanders. I know this because in preparation for my interview with Reykjavík's mayor, Jón Gnarr, I watched several videos of other interviews he'd given previously. In one, he talked about the "Wikings" that came to Iceland. And I'll tell you, it's a good thing I heard him say "Wikings" before meeting him, because I am certain I wouldn't have been able to suppress a giggle if I'd first heard him say it in my interview.

So Route 1 does not have an office but a wan. Car Rental Guy and I go to the wan, sort of a camper wan, really, where he gets me all hooked up. When I made my reservation online, I had declined all the extra types of insurance a person can get — gravel insurance, ash insurance, Super Duper Extra Insurance, etc. — but in my weary state, Car Rental Guy talks me into gravel and Super Duper. Who knows. He does say he doesn't really think ash insurance is necessary, although I swear to you instead of saying "ash," he said "ass." At any rate, my ass is uninsured for the duration of the trip.

Car Rental Guy gives me a very thorough rundown of the car and the insurance and my rental, and then he pulls out the Big Map. (This is not a euphemism; it's really a map. It's a big map, and right on the front, it says, "Big Map.") He then suggests places to see, circling them on the map as he goes: Grindavík, Fimmvörðuháls, Skaftafell, Jökulsárlón. In the north, he circles Dettifoss, Húsavík, Ásbyrgi, Mývatn. On a scrap piece of paper, he writes "Places: Silfra at Þingvellir, Kerið."

He mentions Lagarfljót in the east, to which I reply, "home of the worm!" Car Rental Guy looks at me with a bit of surprise and a bit of delight.

"Not many people know about the worm," he says with what I'm sure was a touch of admiration. The Lagarfljót Worm is Iceland's Loch Ness Monster; it's said to be a football field long, with many humps. It's been noted in literature since the 1300s. So it must be real! Supposedly sightings of The Worm portend natural disaster, so I guess I'm hoping not to see it. But I'll drive by on my route. I nod as he writes down: Lagarfljót.

And then, with no great hug or anything to commemorate the intimate time we'd just spent together, the thoughts on Iceland we'd shared, the moments we'll always cherish, we parted ways.

A few thoughts about car rental: When I first started thinking about coming to Iceland, I investigated car rental prices and was a bit shocked at the cost, but I mentally prepared myself and added it to the budget. Then, for a variety of reasons, I didn't make my reservation. When I finally got around to it, at the beginning of June (for an end of July/beginning of August reservation), the prices seemed to have doubled. Ack! I about had an apoplectic shock at that time. It then occurred to me that a place like Iceland, where tourism is growing, has a finite number of cars, and when they're gone they're gone. I realize that's true of all places, but in my mind it makes sense, right? I mean, if you're in Washington, there could be cars coming and going from Oregon or Idaho or even Canada. But Iceland is pretty isolated. What it has is more or less what it has. (The rental companies do note you may not take their cars out of Iceland. I found this quite amusing until they mentioned the ferry to Norway. Okay, check, not planning to go to Norway, and not planning to drive into the ocean, so we're good.)

At that point, I bit the bullet and quickly made my reservation before prices could go up any more. Then, a few weeks later, in a last-ditch hope to find better prices, I tried again. I found Route 1, which had better prices than what I'd already reserved and had availability in the car I wanted, so I canceled my first reservation and went with Route 1. They've been very good with questions over email, and Car Rental Guy, though a little late in finding me, was quite nice. So far, so good.

So I'm on the road, the sun is out, the sky is huge, my GPS is programmed for my first stop, Blue Lagoon. I'm heading down for an in-water massage. IN-WATER MASSAGE, PEOPLE. What's not to love about the sound of that? I cannot wait.

Now here, I must tell you, it is indeed my instinct to call this spa of luxury and hot waters "*the* Blue Lagoon" rather than "Blue Lagoon," but I looked it up and they don't use "the" on their website so that's what I'm going with, no matter how weird it sounds. But it sounds weird, right? It's not just me?

Anyhoo, driving along the road to Blue Lagoon, I am fascinated by the landscape: a vast, barren lava field. Truly, not that I've been on the moon, but this is what you might imagine parts of the moon might look like, if the lava rocks on the moon were also covered with a licheny mossy plant of some sort. The moss almost looks like it would look if you took that fire extinguisher foam, colored it a light gray-green, and sprayed it over the rocks. Just a light coating, barely a hint of life amongst the barrenness. The terrain, flat and treeless, stretches out as far as the eye can see. After not too long, ahead of me and to the right I see steam rising out from the ground. "That must be Blue Lagoon," I think, and sure enough, it is. On a clear day like today, you can see it from at least five miles away. Coming from Seattle, home of trees and hills, this landscape is, indeed, foreign.

I have this thing, this mental issue, this self-delusion. When I'm planning trips, I spend so much time looking at maps that I get this false sense that I'll easily be able to drive or maneuver wherever I'm going. It's like I somehow imagine I'll still be able to look down on the landscape from above and see all the roads neatly labeled, like somehow I'll manage to keep my directions straight, north from east from south from west, and won't ever get turned around, like I won't miss roads and turns. Realizing that I can see Blue Lagoon from miles away perhaps perpetuates this false sense of hope. Maybe, for once, in this flat, treeless landscape, I will be able to not get lost.

The spa opens at 9 a.m. Normally the first in-water massage is at 11, but today a masseuse happens to be coming in at 10, so a few weeks ago I booked this first massage of the day. When I arrive at 9:30, only a few cars are in the parking lot, plus a couple small vans. "No crowds at all!" I think to myself. I've heard the place can be mobbed, but as I drive up, all is serene.

I can see bits of Blue Lagoon water as I head into the complex, before I'm even parked, little riverlets on the side of the road. This water is actually blue. Not clear, like water normally is, but blue. It is a rich, opaque, milky, gorgeous, calming turquoise blue like you never thought water could be, the edges of the water in the waterways fringed a bright mineral-white from the silica and sulfur. Looking at it is a spa treatment for my eyes. I park, and before I walk inside the complex, I walk around the building to the left a bit and discover some of the pools (all man-made, by the way). When I peek at these pools, no one is there. Not realizing these are not the bathing pools, I think I've hit the jackpot: Blue Lagoon is mine alone. I feel welcomed and embraced by the warmth of the hot springs and the country.

Of course I'm wrong, those are just extra pools, for show, I suppose. I go in, get my special bracelet that serves as a lock for my locker, shower (you must shower before entering and after exiting), and head to the massage area. The sun dazzles bright. The sky is cloudless. I feel refreshed just looking at the pools (which do actually have people in them, but at this point, not too many).

Eventually, just a couple minutes late, my masseuse shows up. She directs me to hop onto a sort of pool float, and covers me with a warm, wet towel. "I am wondering about your swimsuit top," she says. "Can you put it to your hips? You are covered with a towel."

Oh sure. What the heck. I felt very much on public display, but also very tired and very relaxed and very unconcerned.

She proceeds. She oils up my feet and starts massaging them, at which point I realize how tired my feet are. She continues up my legs, arms, neck, shoulders, and finally near the end of my hour-long massage she's pouring warm oil into my hair and giving me a scalp massage. Through it all I am resting, reminding myself to relax, reminding myself I don't have to actually consciously relax but rather I should let myself relax, reminding myself that I don't have to use this free time to solve the problems of the world in my mind. I let my mind wander into nothingness. I watch the sky change from blue, to blue with a few clouds, to blue with clouds like an endless sheet of cottonballs that someone pulled apart to expose the fluffy side. Life is good.

And then the massage is over. I don't have time to dawdle, really, so I don't partake of the silica mud that you can put on your face, but I hear it's lovely for the skin. The silica in the water is not, however, lovely for the hair, especially in combination with massage oil. Despite a shower with lots of shampoo and conditioner, as I leave Blue Lagoon my hair is a matted rat's nest. The shower rooms have filled to overflowing with naked women fresh off tour buses, women in all states of undress, showering and trying to find open hooks for their towels and looking for the pools. One poor attendant gently reminds people not to walk past a certain point without drying off first, and then laboriously mops up after all those who don't listen. What started off as serene has become, frankly, a bit of a madhouse, and is making me slightly claustrophobic. I am sticky and a little too warm getting back into my clothes. The experience itself was relaxing, but the combination of too many people as I left and not feeling clean ended my visit on an odd note.

It's after 11:30 now, and suddenly I worry I'm a little behind schedule. I look at my eleven-page itinerary to see what I've scheduled next: Öndverðarnes. It should be to the east of the airport, more or less. There's a lighthouse there, if I recall correctly. My oh-so-thorough itinerary is not nearly as thorough as it should be, and I realize I didn't write down why I wanted to go to Öndverðarnes. All I know is that it is important enough I decided I should go there. So I type it into my GPS, tediously: "Ondver...," and decide to let the GPS finish it from there, tell me all the places it can find starting with Ondver.

It knows nothing.

COME ON. I try with just "Ond."

Still, nothing.

I am too tired to problem-solve, so I mentally cross that one off the list. I can see lighthouses anywhere.

The order for the rest of the day, as planned, is this: Gullfoss, Öxarárfoss, Þingvellir. However, I can no longer remember why I decided to travel the destinations in this order. Was it related to the location of Öndverðarnes? If I head to Gullfoss, I'll pass right through Þingvellir. I decide to just stop at Þingvellir first.

And here, I think, is a good place to begin our Icelandic language lessons.

So, while in Icelandic it's Þingvellir, you'll often see the name written as Thingvellir. The Þ (or þ in lower case) is pronounced sort of like "th." Just to add to the confusion, though, there's also Ð/ð, which is also pronounced more or less like "th." Car Rental Guy explained to me that words never start with Ð/ð, so you really only will see ð unless the word is written in all caps.

Then there's Æ/æ, which Car Rental Guy told me is pronounced like "eye." The letter "i" is pronounced ... well, I want to say it's like "e." I could be wrong. There's also ö, á, é, í, ó, ú, and ý, in addition to all their un-accented counterparts, and I have no idea how those are pronounced. As for words, I know these few: vík = creek; foss = waterfall; jökull = glacier. And as far as I can tell, if there are two Ls together, as in Eyjafjallajökull, the volcano that blew recently, I think the two Ls are pronounced sort of like tl or dl. So Eyjafjallajökull has a bit of a fyadl and a bit of jokudl in it. I think? And Þingvellir is sort of Thingvettlir. We will see as the trip progresses. Stay tuned.

Oh, one more. The Lagarfljót Worm is Lagarfljótsormur — except, CRG told me, because it is THE Lagarfljót Worm rather than A Lagarfljót Worm, it is Lagarfljótsormurinn. The "inn" on the end indicates that something is the THE of something, the only one or the most important one. If that makes sense. I mean it does. So there you go.

Þingvellir is a National Park, and it's stunning. This is where the rift between the North American and European plates can be seen pulling apart. This pulling apart is not just one line, the ground on the left pulling away from the ground on the right, not one single long crevice as some people think it might be or should be; rather, it's sort of an area of land that all just keeps breaking up. Sort of like stretch marks for the Earth, only a lot prettier. I drive into the park and stop at different stops to see what can be seen, starting with the visitor centre and a viewing spot at Hakið. The ground separating from itself has created long crevasses and caverns, clefts and chasms, with deep, crystal-clear deep green-blue pools at their bases, the water so clear that in some places you have to look twice to know it's there.

Þingvellir is also historically one of the most important places in Iceland, as it's the place where the Icelandic parliament was founded more than a thousand years ago. From 930 to nearly 1800 C.E., Icelanders gathered yearly at Þingvellir to recite and enact laws, decide disputes, and discuss matters of importance to all the people. The Alþingi, or Icelandic parliament, is one of the oldest parliamentary institutions in the world.

I meander along the roads in the park until I find another spot to stop. As it turns out, I'm now at an area near the Þingvallakirkja church. I saw this church just a few minutes ago, from above, when I was looking down from the Hakið viewing spot, which is now far above and across a river. I see an Icelandic flag and later realize it marks the spot of the Lögberg, or Law Rock, the place where the Alþingi was first held in 930 C.E. Trails from both my current spot and down from Hakið lead visitors to Lögberg, but not knowing this at the time, I move along.

A note of interest: Game of Thrones, the TV show based on the bestselling books, is filming here at Þingvellir right now, and indeed has been here for two weeks, or so I've heard through the grapevine known as social media. After a brief search I find them, out near Öxarárfoss, the waterfall on the Öxará river that was on my list of places to visit. They're actually right next to Drekkingar-hylur — the "drowning pool," which, legend has it, was used back in the day to drown women who were adulterous or needed to be punished for some other reason (men got their heads chopped off instead). It looks like they're filming at the pool! They need extras! They need female extras whose hair looks like it's been matted and tangled, as if she's just been at Blue Lagoon, and got both Blue Lagoon water and massage oil in her hair — very medieval, you know! They ask me to be a part of the show! They have an extra costume in just my size! I'll be paid $700 just for showing up at the right time!

Or, alternatively, in my jet-lagged stupor, I completely forget to look for Öxarárfoss, which I'd totally meant to do, and I never see the Game of Thrones people, and I don't even remember it until later the next day. One or the other. I'm not telling. You'll have to guess.

Then, my GPS decides to mess with me. I'm driving along, having set the GPS now for Gullfoss, and I reach a corner. The map on my GPS clearly shows an upcoming right turn, but then the map abruptly flips and twirls on the screen, and the GPS voice tells me with great confidence to turn left. I turn left, and end up looping around roads I'd already driven. It adds a half hour to my drive, but I am enjoying the beauty of the area and just take it in stride. I drive along, but I am getting tired. Very tired. The roads in Iceland, outside the cities, are quite narrow, and I can't let my attention wander, which would be far too easy to do in my overly tired state. About half an hour from Gullfoss, I decide I am simply too tired to be driving anymore. My adventures for the day have already taken far longer than I'd planned, and it's getting late in the day, but I'm only half an hour away from the waterfall. It would be ridiculous to turn around. So I find a picnic site, pull in, put my seat back, and sleep for about twenty minutes until I wake up. I'm momentarily confused about where I am, but soon enough I'm back on track. The short nap is enough to revitalize me, and off to Gullfoss I go.

Gullfoss, like Þingvellir, is one of three main stops on the Golden Circle. Before we go any further, let's discuss the concept of "Golden Circle," shall we?

I guarantee that the moment you start researching a trip to Iceland, you will be unable to avoid reading about The Golden Circle. Every tour company has a Golden Circle tour, it seems. It's everywhere. The Golden Circle is basically a very popular tourist route that includes three key Iceland attractions: Þingvellir; the Gullfoss waterfall; and the valley of Haukadalur, which is primarily significant for the geyser named Geysir, and also for the geyser Strokkur, for reasons I shall address later.

Now, I realize I have the perhaps somewhat rare distinction of being both daughter and granddaughter of math teachers, but does it not bother anyone else that they are calling three points a "circle"? Clearly, clearly three points define a triangle, not a circle. One point, a point. Two points, a line. Three points, a triangle. I mean, I know it's been a long time since I last stepped into a math classroom, but isn't that right?

Of course I understand it's not just about the points themselves; it's about the route. Perhaps that's what the "circle" part of The Golden Circle refers to, the route. The route one travels to see these three sites must be more or less circular, shall we assume? Let's see …

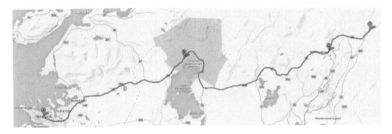

Oh.

Well then.

Anyway, "Gullfoss" means "Golden Waterfall," so at least there's that.

(I'll note that there's also a "Diamond Circle," up in north Iceland. Diamond Circle. Don't even get me started.)

Perhaps because Þingvellir is so spread out, it didn't feel inundated by tourists. Gullfoss, however, is crowded. I park a good distance from the visitor centre, and note that there don't seem to be many spots left in the parking area. A steady stream of people is walking to and from the waterfall, pouring out of giant tour buses and climbing back in. I get in step with those heading down the path to the falls. It's a short hike to the viewing point, which then branches out to a few different trails. To my right are stairs down to a lower level. Like flies to honey, if there are stairs, I must climb (or in this case, descend) them. I'm already being assaulted by the enormous spray from this powerful waterfall and its two-tiered cascade. My camera lens is quickly covered in tiny water drops, and I'm grateful my aunt thought to lend me her lens-cleaning tools. I wipe my lens several times while I'm there, trying to get pictures, but in the end it's a losing battle. The spray wins.

The waterfall is gorgeous. The Hvítá river ("white river") gush-es widely downstream over a three-stepped staircase, and then drops eleven meters and then plunges another twenty-one meters deep into a crevice; this combination of drops makes up what is known as Gullfoss. Visitors view the waterfall from the top level, off to the side, and from this viewpoint the crevice looks deep, like it could take you to the center of the Earth. The enormous volume of water creates an overpowering roar; the air itself becomes part of the waterfall.

I watch from the lower level for a while, then walk back up the stairs and out a trail to get a different view. The sound of the water is all encompassing and leaves me with a strange sensation, like I'm in a cocoon where no other sound can enter, nothing but the never-ending crash of the falls. The spray intensifies as I get closer, and soon I realize if I continue, I'll be drenched. I head back to my car with the throngs of other tourists to continue on my way.

Despite my earlier nap, I'm still very tired. It's nearing 4 p.m., my hosts (my friend Mary Frances and her family) are expecting me around 5, I haven't slept since the dawn of time, and the drive "home" will take an hour and a half. Golden Waterfall, second on the Golden Circle: check.

Now, I had not really planned to visit Geysir, I'll admit it. Geysers in general don't thrill me, and I'd heard that Geysir (the geyser after which all other geysers are named) got itself all plugged up by decades or centuries or millennia of people throwing things into it, and is not particularly spectacular after all this time. More showy at this point is its neighbor geyser, Strokkur, Icelandic for "churn," which erupts every four to eight minutes, blasting from fifteen to twenty meters high, sometimes even up to forty meters.

But when I told Car Rental Guy that I wasn't going to go to Geysir, he laughed. "It's just across the street from Gullfoss," he told me, "so if you are going to Gullfoss you may as well go to Geysir."

It's not exactly across the street, but it is on the same road, he's right about that. As I head back toward Reykjavík, I'm still debating whether to stop. But then, you may remember how I could see Blue Lagoon from five miles away? In the same manner, as I'm driving along I suddenly see a geyser — not sure which one, but probably Stokkur — erupt, at least a mile or two away from where I am. "Geysir: check," I think. I am satisfied that I have seen the Golden Circle, and I head to meet my friend at her home in Reykjavík.

Along the way, I have to stop one more time for one more twenty-minute nap. This was an insanely full day for a first day in a time zone seven hours after my own with no sleep, but I am glad to have made the most of my time. I have much to do while I'm here. No time to waste!

I drive straight on to Reykjavík, and maneuver through the city traffic well enough with the help of the more-or-less trusty GPS. When I arrive at Mary Frances's, she is waiting with a warm meal for me, a shower in which to scrub off two days of weariness, and a room to sleep. A home.

What I'd do differently on my next visit:

Þingvellir was gorgeous, peaceful, and powerful. If it's possible to feel the energy of the Earth and of the past, I'd say you can feel it there. You could easily spend a day or more walking around in the park, exploring trails and waterfalls, especially if the weather is as lovely as it was for me today. Every day in the summer, park rangers take visitors on free hour-long guided tours that tell you all about the story of Þingvellir both geologically and as a place of assembly for nearly a thousand years. The area attracts nearly 300,000 visitors each year, and for good reason. I would have loved more time there.

In addition, Silfra, which Car Rental Guy mentioned, sounds incredible. It's located in Lake Þingvallavatn (another Icelandic lesson: vatn=water, I believe), Iceland's largest lake. The clear waters supposedly give amazing visibility for scuba diving or snorkeling, and it's listed as one of the top three diving destinations in the world. This is something I would have learned about, I am sure, if I'd had my usual amount of time to plan for my trip, and I regret that I didn't plan more time here to snorkel a bit in this amazing tectonic rift.

When I was at Blue Lagoon, a couple came by who were spending only twenty-four hours in Iceland. They'd already been down to Grindavík (on the same road as that to Blue Lagoon; just keep going), and said it was quaint and fabulous with a wonderful little bakery, and I should go down. With a full schedule already planned, I skipped it, but it would be something to look into.

Also, I've just learned about the geothermal area at Krýsuvík, and the nearby Lake Kleifarvatn hot springs, including, perhaps, a recently discovered underwater hot spring? I don't know much, but would look that up if I were coming again.

Reykjavík to Vík

Wednesday, July 31, 2013

Either that futon I slept on last night was the most comfortable bed ever created in the history of beds and all humankind, or I was exhausted. Having gone non-stop yesterday, I slept like a baby. I've brought along an eye mask to help me sleep, should the midnight sun get to me. (Right now Iceland has about four hours of "darkness" at night, though I'm told it never really gets dark these days.) I tested the mask at home, though, and both times I slept with it on I (1) had weird dreams about my eyes being sliced open, and (2) woke up with a gnarly sense of dehydration in my nose and eyes. So I'm delighted that Mary Frances has "blackout curtains" on the windows in the bedrooms, which more or less block the sunlight, except a bit around the edges. Regardless, I slept pretty well. I woke up once around 3 a.m., saw the light peeking out from behind the curtain, looked at my phone to see if it was time to get up, and went back to sleep.

While in Reykjavík — that is, last night, and again for a few nights at the end of my trip — I'm staying with Mary Frances, a friend I once worked with in Seattle. She's a Washington native, but one fateful day many years ago in Seattle she met her future husband. He's Icelandic, but was at school at the University of Washington. They met on a bus, and the rest is history. Mary Frances moved to Iceland five years ago and now is fluent in Icelandic, but says it's a very hard language to learn. Her children, a two-year-old and a three-year-old, are learning both English and Icelandic, and can switch between the two with ease. (Well, at least the three-year-old can; the two-year-old is a two-year-old after all, but it's clear he has both languages in him as well.) It's a bit amazing to witness.

We start the day off lazily, chatting about life and the world and Icelandic politics. Then, they are off to play and I am off to drive around the country. My adventure begins.

I must attend to a few orders of business before I head out into the country. Yesterday, I saw both a giant tour bus and a car flapping along the roads with flat tires, as well as another car randomly stranded on the side of the road. I'm slightly uneasy about my travel now, since I'll be on these roads all alone. Seeing how there is so much land between places in Iceland sometimes, I'd already decided I'd get a cheap phone to have with me in case of emergency. (FYI: I've done this in other countries before, but have never been sure whether the phones will work if I take them somewhere else, so I've just bought several new phones over the years.)

I stop at a mall in Reykjavík and scan a mall directory for a phone store. It's at this time that I realize I don't know the Icelandic words for "phone store." I head to the nearest booth and ask for help. A young man points me to the ladies at the Information desk, who in turn point me up the stairs to the phone store. I pick out the cheapest phone, and the clerk tells me this phone will work anywhere (I assume anywhere in Europe, but he could really mean anywhere, like even Mars); I just need to go to a phone store and buy a SIM card in each country I visit. I notice that my phone number has a 666 in it, and hope that's not foreshadowing. Local Icelandic phone: check.

Next, I need to fill up the car with gas.

Let's talk about this a bit. In the U.S., most of our credit cards don't have what's called a "chip-and-PIN" — that is, a card with a chip embedded in it (microchip, not potato chip), and a PIN associated with the card, for security. In Europe (and elsewhere, too, maybe? I haven't looked it up), the credit cards all have chip-and-PIN, so machines that take credit cards are built with the expectation that your card will have a chip-and-PIN. If your credit card is chipless and PINless (like mine are), you will face some difficulties — especially at gas stations. (Note: Some U.S. cards are chip-and-signature but not chip-and-PIN.)

My favorite Car Rental Guy had given me a little map that shows all the Orkan and Shell stations in Iceland, explaining that I could get a discount by using a key card he gave me. "Orkan is cheapest," he'd said. "At Shell you pay more for 'services' but those services really aren't anything." At the time I didn't really know what he meant, but I've asked my GPS to guide me to the nearest Orkan, and as I pull in, I think I understand. The Orkan stations are as simple as can be: just a few pumps out in the middle of nowhere. No store, no attendants, just you, your car, a pump. And your credit card, which may or may not have chip-and-PIN. And instructions on the pump screen in Icelandic.

That's not entirely true. I manage to get the first few instructions in English. Since my debit card has a PIN at least, I decide I'll try using that. I type it in, and then … something in Icelandic comes up on the screen. Clearly I have been rejected, but I don't know why.

There's an older gentleman using the other Orkan pump.

"Excuse me," I call out, "Do you speak English?"

He does. They all do, which is so helpful.

He comes over and watches as I put the card in again, go through the instructions again. He reads the final rejection notice to me, the one in Icelandic.

"It says you do not have clearance to use this card."

I don't?

"Do you have another card?" he asks.

"I do, but it doesn't have chip or PIN."

He nods. He knows what my problem is, but he encourages me to try anyway.

Rejected, again.

And so, I thank the kind gas station guy, get back in my car, and ask my GPS to get me to a Shell station, where I'm guessing the "services" include the ability for me to walk inside a store and get help from a live person.

I am correct in this assumption. I pull up, and walk inside the gas station store.

"I don't have a chip-and-PIN on my credit card," I say. "Can I still get gas here?"

"Yes, I will open the pump, then you can pay inside when you are done."

I tell him what pump I'm on — number six — and go outside, pump gas, and come back in to pay. I make a mental note to always try to get gas during open hours. I don't want to end up somewhere low on gas but with no one around to help.

I'm about to get on my way out of town when I see a "Bónus" store, which looks suspiciously like it might have food inside. I go in and find my suspicions confirmed. It's sort of a no-frills super-market, cheaper than some other stores, I'm told. I buy some Skyr — Icelandic yogurt, which, from what I've heard, is akin to nectar for the gods or some such thing. I try it and it is, indeed, quite tasty. Having expected to reach Nirvana through Skyr, though, I'm the tiniest bit disappointed. It's quite good, but not transcendental. Perhaps I got the wrong flavor?

And finally, just before noon, I'm on my way.

Today, I'm planning to drive from Reykjavík to the southern coastal town of Vík, with a number of stops along the way, including several waterfalls. Noting that yesterday I had clearly overestimated how much I can fit into one day, I study my list to see what is essential and what is not. Háifoss is supposed to be my first stop: I've noted "waterfall and land formations." I haven't printed off a map and can't find it quickly on my Big Map, but I seem to recall it was a little out of the way. I will see lots of waterfalls. Háifoss is off the itinerary.

Next on the list, then: Keldur. "Turf houses," I've noted — finally I've remembered to make a note on my itinerary explaining why I want to go somewhere. Yes! I remember this. I found Keldur early in my Iceland research and have been looking forward to the turf houses, have seen them in many pictures online and can't wait to get my own pictures. This sounds good. I type Keldur into my GPS.

My GPS has no idea what I'm talking about.

All right then. Note: When you write things down when you're planning your trip, don't forget all the accent marks. To me, Myvatn is basically the same as Mývatn, but it's not to my GPS. (They are also basically the same to Google, which I think is part of the problem; while planning my trip I became complacent about those silly little accent marks, not realizing they might actually matter.) I think this could be what caused my problem yesterday with Öndverðarnes (or maybe not, too late now), but Keldur is just Keldur. This I know for sure. My GPS refuses to find Keldur, and I am discouraged. (The lesson: If you write place-names down, write down some alternatives. Knowing what I know now, if I were going back, I'd also note the church, Keldnakirkja, or I'd note that it was out Rangárvallavegur/264, which I believe is "Rangárvalla Road." My GPS still might not have found it but at least I'd have had more information to help me find it with or without the GPS.)

Keldur looks fabulous online, but I won't be seeing it today. I wish I could have found it. If you go and find it, send pictures.

As for me, I move on.

While I was searching for Keldur, I went so far as to type in simply "Ke" to see what the GPS could find. (A somewhat pointless exercise, as I don't want to go to the wrong thing and end up a hundred miles in the wrong direction. Place names can be very similar in Iceland, so you have to be really careful.) Kerið was on the list, and I remember that Car Rental Guy mentioned it yesterday. A crater, I remember, often included as part of the Golden Circle. What the heck. I set the course into the GPS and head off.

Kerið is easy enough to find. I pull into the parking lot, open my car door, and …

So, somewhere in all the things I read there was a comment about high winds in Iceland. Someone warned that when you get out of your car, you should hang on to the door, as a high wind might come along just at that moment and with great force fling your door into the car or person or cliff or whatever is next to you.

Thankfully, there is no car or person or cliff next to where I've parked, because that there was a strong wind. Thankfully, the car door itself does not get snapped off with this intense gust. With a bit of effort I push the door shut, then head to my trunk where I've packed my coat in the top of one bag. With the wind working against me, I struggle to even get my coat on. My hair has become a weapon of mass destruction, whipping into my mouth and eyes and back again. I turn to face into the wind, trying to get my hair to fly behind me, so that I can gather it into a hairband. So much for styling my hair. The wind is furious and although the day isn't cold, the wind chill is. There's a tiny bit of rain, but there's no way an umbrella would stand up to this. I pay my entrance fee — about $3 — and walk up to the crater.

The wind is so fierce it's thrashing everyone's clothes around them, shirts and coats and pant legs, every loose bit of clothing has declared an assault on its associated body. The air is thick with the sound of flapping fabric, fighting to be freed to fly off into the wind.

The crater is interesting, beautiful, and there's a trail around to the left and down to the lake where one can follow to get a closer look, but I have had enough of the wind. It isn't raining much but the wind has turned the tiny drops into stinging pellets. "I miss trees," I think. "Iceland, a wind tunnel," I think. The deep turquoise of the lake, its surface rippling furiously in the wind; the rich red lava of the steep slopes of the crater with black lava peeking through in areas; the gentle grassy green on one side; all these become secondary to the dominant thought: "This wind is going to push me over the edge into the crater, and I will die." There are no barriers, no railings, which is a wonderful change of pace from the United States. I firmly believe in common sense, and if one does not have the common sense to use one's common sense, then there are consequences. On the other hand, I have no desire to plummet to my death, to be a personal witness to how it would feel to tumble down the side of a volcanic crater.

Pictures, then back to the car.

Today, the roads I'm driving on are not all as nicely paved as they were yesterday. Car Rental Guy talked me into the gravel insurance, and I'd wondered if I was being a fool in accepting it. However, I hit my first gravel road today, and am very glad for his wisdom. Even at the low speed of about 25 miles per hour, gravel is flying. I'd say overall the extra insurance is worth it. It's not that driving is any harder here, really, than at home; it's that the margin for error is so much smaller. I don't know who was in charge of making the roads in Iceland, but they are very narrow, and most of them are at least slightly elevated from the surrounding area (meaning if you go off the road, you plunge down into the floor of Iceland), and there is practically no shoulder. None. Nada. (Which also makes it all but impossible to stop on the side of the road anywhere to take awesome pictures of awesome sights, which also sucks.) I know some people aren't comfortable about the idea of driving alone around a country, but I figure I drove two weeks around Scotland once, on the other side of the road, and I drove a week or so in Ireland and Northern Ireland, solo, on the other side of the road, so I can handle anything, right? But I'll tell you, driving in Iceland can be tiring, because as I said you really have to concentrate. If you see that pretty thing on the side of the road, across the distance, that waterfall cascading down the shelf from the highlands, you have to glance very fast because if your attention wanders it will take hardly any time at all for your car to slip off the non-shoulder into the ditch. And undoubtedly, aside from the time and effort to wait for someone to come along and help you, that would call into play the deductible on the car, and no one wants that. So if you come to Iceland, be prepared for the roads. I don't want to discourage anyone from driving here, but I do think it's good to know what you're getting into. And Iceland, maybe think about improving — especially widening — the roads a bit? Just a suggestion!

On to the first waterfall of the day: Seljalandsfoss. This is one of Iceland's most famous waterfalls, and certainly is worthy of the honor. It's beautiful. Here, if you don't mind getting drenched, you can actually walk behind the waterfall itself. That is, I should add, if you also don't mind your camera getting wet. I start off to walk behind the falls, but the spray fills the air long before I'm even near the falls. I bought my camera new for this trip and do not want to ruin it so quickly. Besides which, I have a good ways to drive yet and even in the short distance I walk I can feel the water seeping through my clothes. I back off and admire the waterfall from farther away.

Off a bit to the left of Seljalandsfoss, I see another, smaller waterfall, so I walk down the path to explore. Soon I notice that the hillside has what looks suspiciously like stairs carved into the dirt, leading up to a small cave just to the right of the smaller waterfall. I stare at the stairs. They are calling to me. Sometimes I think I may have been a mountain goat in a former lifetime, because just as with the stairs at Gullfoss yesterday, I can't help but think that things that can be climbed, should be climbed. As I ponder the steep, muddy hillside, a young man with the same idea but less caution starts up the hill. I decide to watch him and see what happens. He makes it up about halfway the richly green hillside before he stops. At first I think he's unable to find any further path, but then I realize his father is calling to him from below to pause for a picture. Then, a young woman — a sister? a girlfriend? — starts up after him. I see another woman watching them, not far from me. I'd seen her with the father earlier, so I'm guessing this is the mother. I move closer to her, smile, and say, "It'll be much harder to get down, I think!"

"On bottom," she says with a laugh and a thick accent (Italian?), indicating her suspicion, which I share, that they'll find themselves sliding down the muddy way.

The young kids take their time getting up and down the hill, so I wander back to the parking lot, looking over my shoulder once or twice. Sure enough, down proves more difficult than up. The kids (they're probably in their late teens or even early twenties, but you know, age is relative) are staring down the hill and realizing they may have gotten themselves into something that they can't get out of; at least, not without a giant wet dirt stains on their behinds. It would have been fun to climb up the hill, but I'm glad I decided not to.

Skógafoss is next. An interesting note about the coastline of Iceland: Over the millennia, ages, eons, or some other long span of time, Iceland's coastline has receded a few miles from its former location, and now there's a sort of "shelf" a few miles in from and parallel to the current coastline. All the houses and roads and everything else sit at a level far below the shelf. In essence, when you drive along the Ring Road in the south (I'm not sure how far this extends, but I know for sure it's in part of the south), you're driving on what was once the ocean floor. As a result of this fabulous geological change, you can see dozens — hundreds — thousands of waterfalls cascading down from this shelf, some more grand and spectacular than others, such as Seljalandsfoss and Skógafoss, but still, there are waterfalls everywhere, rivulets running down the cliffside, in one fell swoop or in several steps. I remind myself to keep my eyes on the road but at some points it seems anywhere you look, you're within viewing distance of some spectacular waterfall, large or small.

And horses, too. When I first started researching Iceland I learned of the famous Icelandic horses, sometimes referred to as ponies because they're smaller than "regular" horses. These were first brought over by Scandinavian settlers more than a thousand years ago, and are now a most sturdy breed, long-lived and hardy, and they are pure. If a horse leaves Iceland, it's not allowed to return; non-Icelandic horses are not allowed to enter the country. So when I was planning this trip, I thought to myself that I must make a point to be sure to see the horses.

No need to make the effort. The horses are everywhere. It occurs to me, even, that there are far more horses than there can possibly be demand for horse riding. What does this mean? These horses, some of them at least, must be for … eating. Hmm.

So I'm driving along, thinking about horses, and as always the roads are narrow and there's no where to pull over. In fact, there are so few spots at which to pull over that I've noticed when someone else has pulled over, everyone else looks to see what was worth the effort. This is the case a short while before Skógafoss. I see that coming up on the left, two cars have pulled over. What is the draw? I spot it immediately: There's some sort of cave, but clearly it's been made into a shelter by humans. It looks a little like a Hobbit home. Definitely worth exploring!

I drive until I'm able to pull into a turn-around. The two cars behind me do the same. We all head back to the cave.

I park, climb through a gate, then carefully pick my way through the grass — this is sheep territory, and the grass is tall, meaning, it could hide the sheep deposits and I wouldn't know I'd stepped in one until I smelled it back in the car. I walk up to the cave, and am transported back in time. According to a placard at the site, this cave is one of only ninety such caves in the south of Iceland, and they don't seem to appear anywhere else in the country. This one is named Rútshellir — Rútur's Cave. (If you want to search out some of the other caves in the area, look up Paradísarhellir and Steinahellir.) Rútshellir is, they say, the oldest surviving man-made residence in Iceland. Part of the cave is boarded up. I meander close, but not too close. I've watched too many episodes of The X-Files to go inside. I've heard that there are a substantial number of Icelanders who believe in elves. While I suspect that's a "fact" invented to draw the tourists, I am smart enough to know that if there are elves, they are inside this cave. And what do I know of elves? I haven't studied them. Undoubtedly they're mischievous. Likely they enjoy scaring the crap out of people traveling solo. I wander around the cave, then shake off the magical otherworldly aura that lingers around the place and head back to my car.

Is that the smell of sheep in the car with me? I decide it's just my imagination, but make a note to wipe my shoes diligently at the next stop.

Onward to Skógafoss. Another of Iceland's most famous waterfalls and one of its largest, this one has an element of legend to it. The stories say that Þrasi Þórólfsson (remember that Þ is pronounced Th), the first Viking settler in the area, buried a treasure chest behind the waterfall. Years later, a young local boy found the chest, but he was only able to grab a ring on the side of the chest before it disappeared. Supposedly the ring was then given to the local church, and now the ring has its home at the Skógar Folk Museum. True? Just a myth? Who knows?

Regardless of the legend of the ring, I notice that next to Skógafoss is a trail leading up the hill, with flight after flight after flight of stairs. Did I mention that if there are stairs, I must climb them? My feet guide me to the bottom of the stairs and I begin climbing. And counting, too, because that's part of the rules: You climb, and you count.

When I'm about two hundred twenty steps up and taking a break, a woman climbing down from the top sees me and stops.

"There's not much up there," she says.

I look at the top of the stairs. But … I must climb. But … this is a lot of stairs. I'm only about halfway, I estimate.

"No," she continues, "my son ran up to the top and he says all you can see is a little bit of the waterfall, and the river."

I look up. I look down.

"Okie dokie," I say, and down I go again.

So I can't tell you whether, in fact, all you can see from the top is a little bit of the waterfall and the river, but I can tell you it's a misty day and the view would not have been too expansive today. I am satisfied with my decision and make my way back to the base of the waterfall to admire it a bit longer.

Now, the thing with sights is that it's really easy to look at them and say: "Skógafoss: check," and move on. I'm feeling the pressure of my long list of sights to see and the long drives I've planned each day, but I want to make sure I do more than check sights off a to-see list. So I stand at the edge of the shallow rock-strewn river at the base of Skógafoss and focus on the waterfall, stand with my eyes closed and listen, look around me to absorb the site. The red-roofed houses on the other side of the river, the sheep gently grazing, the grassy slope leading up the hill, the tempting campsite on my side of the river, I soak it all in. Sometimes, such as now, I try to make my mind travel back in time to imagine early settlers here, what they may have been like, imagine them playing and washing in the waterfall's river. I am, therefore, at the site for a while. During this course of time I notice something: waves of visitors. Every time a tour bus arrives, a rush of people comes to the falls, takes pictures, and leaves. Another tour bus, another wave of people. Sometimes, there are short stretches when one busload of people has just left and another has not yet arrived, and it's just us few dozen self-drive people and hiking and biking people, taking our time, but at Skógafoss, there is a constant stream of people. The quieter times between waves are very nice. The rush times disconcert me for some reason, make me uncomfortable, and I'm not quite sure why. Maybe it's the dissonance between the desire to quietly ponder the power and grandeur of the sites, and the cacophony of the crowds of people in a rush to see the sights before their buses leave.

After Skógafoss, my next scheduled stop is Dyrhólaey, a couple dozen kilometers away. As I approach I start to feel I am finally escaping the bus crowds. The Golden Circle felt as crowded as Disneyland, tourists in, tourists out, but this! I am escaping into the Icelandic Outback. Is it the Outback? Is there a word for the Icelandic boonies? They call the center of the island the "highlands," I think, but I don't know if there's a word for the more remote, rural areas of the Ring Road region. Anyway, I feel like I am finally starting to get away. Even my GPS disagrees with me — it tries to send me down another track as I approach Dyrhólaey — surely this means I am about to go into uncharted territory, into a space where no man or woman has boldly gone before?

And then I reach the parking lot.

Three vans.

Well, that's better than the giant buses, anyway.

I take solace in the fact that even if there are three vans, I know I have all the time in the world, and I can wait out any crowds. I walk up paths right and left, taking pictures as I go. The day is still somewhat gray, but the views are spectacular, down the cliffs to the black sand beaches and the mossy-topped lava columns jutting sturdily from the sea, their sides irregular and jagged from the waves. As I look out over some cliffs, a man tells me, "One just flew into its nest." He must think I'm there watching for birds, which tells me there must be birds to be watched there. Possibly puffins, the elusive bird that I'm told is iconic in Iceland though I haven't seen it yet? Or arctic terns, of migratory legend? Regardless, I see none.

I find another path and follow it up to the end of a cliff. Just as I reach the top, the sun starts to come out and I discover I can see a glacier, or a mountain, or a volcano? I'm not sure which. It's beautiful, though, enormous and wide and white and majestic. The clouds shift, and I realize the angle of sunlight is going to be absolutely picture-perfect down on one of the lava columns, so I speed-walk back down to the spot where the man told me about the birds. Sure enough, the angle and nature of the light have brought out the turquoise in the water, lit up the side of the lava column, brightened the yellows and greens, and given me a perfect photo opportunity. With a sigh of satisfaction — right place, right time, right light, never happens! — I snap away. I've noticed already that there are many huge cameras in Iceland. My little Canon SX40 — which feels huge compared to my old camera — is dwarfed by these giants with their long lenses and multiple filters, carried by people whose eyes are constantly scanning the horizon for their next shot. Clearly, Iceland has become a mecca for photographers, and they are everywhere. I wander down one last rocky field and discover a lava bridge. I get down on the ground amongst the rocks, squatting in awkward positions, trying to get pictures of the ocean through the bridge. Two other photographers see me and follow, waiting patiently one after the other for their own chances at the perfect shot.

As I leave, three big buses arrive. Not the biggest, not as big as those on the Golden Circle, but not small. Nothing against tour buses, but today's weather was warm, heavy, muggy. Inside those buses, I know from experience, it is miserable, hot, disgusting. I do not envy those folks.

Next! I've been eagerly awaiting this next place because: hexagonal basalt columns! You may not know of my love for hexagonal basalt columns. I suppose, really, I love any funky, unusual land formation. They're funky and unusual! And hexagonal basalt columns, you don't expect such precise forms in nature, though I don't know why; nature is all about math. Snowflakes and their perfect sides, crystals that form in perfect … uh, crystal form, and pyrite that forms in perfect cubes. So why should hexagonal columns be so surprising? Maybe it's not so much that they're surprising, as it is that they're uncommon. Prior to Iceland, I only knew of the columns at the Giant's Causeway in Northern Ireland, and at the Isle of Staffa in Scotland. (I've visited both, and for my money, I much preferred the Isle of Staffa, but they're spectacular wherever you see them.)

When I first started researching Iceland, I found a place out in the east with hexagonal columns, a waterfall, and I had planned to go way out of my way to see it, just to complete my hexagonal column world visits. But the more I researched, the more I realized Iceland is like the Land of Hexagonal Basalt Columns. The columns are *everywhere*. Proof of this is in the art and architecture you find around Iceland. For example, the design of Hallgrímskirkja, the famous church in downtown Reykjavík, was inspired by these columns.

It makes sense that these columns would be so prevalent. These hexagonal columns are, as I understand it, formed by the rapid cooling of lava after a volcanic eruption. Seeing as Icelandic geological history is all about lava flows (please note I am not a geologist, so this is an imprecise statement, in case you hadn't figured that out), it makes sense that you'd see hexagonal columns everywhere. Many people may come to Iceland for waterfalls, for sheep, for horses, for ice, for hot pools ("hot pots"), for whale watching, for hiking, for many many things, but to be perfectly honest, the idea of all these basalt columns, all over the whole freaking country, got me a little bit excited.

And so, joy in my heart, I head to my penultimate stop of the day, to Reynisfjara (fjara = "beach" when used in a name like this; also means "low tide" or "ebb"), just a bit west of my final destination of Vík. Reynisfjara is a black sand beach, I have read, but, more than that, it is home to grand cathedrals and caverns and caves, all made of hexagonal basalt columns.

The sunshine is quickly fading. As I reach the beach, enshrouded in an increasing fog, Reynisfjara feels like a secret. Even with other people there — not too many — I feel like this place was made for me.

But there's more to Reynisfjara than just the columns, as it turns out. I am delightfully surprised by the beach itself, which is not covered only in black sand. The part where waves meet shore is black sand, but just a bit away from the shoreline, the beach is covered in rocks. Perfect rocks. Gorgeous rocks, of all sizes but in shape they are mostly flat, oval, and smooth. I love rocks, you see. Rocks and I have a thing. Not just because my made-up town in my novels is called Wishing Rock; rather, it's the other way around. My love of rocks made me name a town after one. Is it because they're steady and grounded? Solid and reliable? I don't know, but my rock collection is enough, perhaps, to hold my house down should Seattle ever find itself in the middle of a tornado.

And so, on coming upon Reynisfjara, I feel a bit of joy, as well as a bit of envy, at seeing the assortment of perfect rocks all over the ground, in a thousand various shades of gray. I want them all. I want to take the beach full of rocks home with me. It passes through my mind that perhaps I could gather a few up, but I quickly dismiss the idea. Rocks are not known for being light to carry, after all. I stare at the rocks a bit, knowing we are meant to be together but we never can be. Two ships that pass in the wind. Star crossed lovers. Me and a beach full of beautiful, perfect rocks.

And the columns, of course, are fabulous. If you walk around the curve of the cliff just a short distance, depending on the tide, I'm assuming, there's a wide, somewhat shallow cave. If I lived here, if I had been a kid growing up here, this would have been my secret cave where I and my friends would have conducted secret business in secret. We would have come and made rock monuments that would have been washed away by the waves by the time we came again the next day, so the next day we'd build them again. We'd have claimed certain rocks as our own, and probably assigned names and functions and secret powers to some of the columns. This column is where you make wishes, which will of course come true. That column there is where we eat lunch. These columns here, they lead to another world, if you know the right way to whisper into them. Clearly there is magic here, if you pay enough attention, and listen.

Once, online, I saw someone make fabulous stone art by taking a large oval stone with a bit of a curve to it and putting five smaller oval stones at its top for "toes," making it look like a stone footprint. I gather up some stones that will fit the bill, and perch them on top of a short column, leaving my footprint here, if you will. Just as I'm about to go it starts to rain. The sky is telling me it's time to move on.

Leaving the Reynisfjara area, I stop briefly to capture a photo of the picturesque Reynisfjara church, a traditional Icelandic church with crisp white sides and red roof, with its one pyramidal spire, also topped in red. I'd hoped the sun would come out again to grant me a good picture, but in the fog, the red of the church is intensified, and its misty, mystical aura perfectly suits the land.

I drive away on the quickly dampening road from Reynisfjara, toward my first hotel of the trip, the Hotel Lundi in Vík. This small town has only about three hundred residents, but feels huge in comparison to anything else I've seen all day. When I arrive at the front desk, the man at the desk is charming and sweet, and he invites me to dinner. Technically, he just tells me the hours of the hotel restaurant's dinner, but I know what he meant. I go upstairs, clean up a bit, then come back down to eat.

The dining room is completely full. As I'm asking the waitress about the wait time, though, a man who has been eating alone catches our eyes and indicates he's about to leave. Once he's gone, the table is mine.

I get the menu.

Remember when I was saying earlier that all those horses couldn't be just for riding?

Horse is on the menu.

Now, I decided before I came here that I wasn't going to eat what I define as "gross food." Originally, when I had a travel partner, I had agreed that we'd try the famous Icelandic fermented shark. But my travel partner dropped out and I was off the hook. No gross food for me.

But horse?

Could I eat horse?

The menu does not have extensive options. Horse is on the menu in the form of horseburger. I can handle horseburger, I decide.

Except they have no horseburger tonight. Only horse steak.

What, is there no one in the back with a meat grinder? But I stop with the visual before it goes too far.

So I say yes to the horse steak.

There's WiFi in the hotel and restaurant, so as I eat I am Whatsapping with my parents. (Whatsapp is a texting app that lets you text internationally — I don't know all the details of it except it has proven awesome for us.) They are with my great aunt, back home in Washington, and they tell her I have ordered horse steak. She tells them a story that that back during WWII, she once bought horse meat for dinner, then had unexpected company for the meal. She served the horse meat. No one complained, she says, but they never told anyone it was horse meat, either.

So it's edible, I suppose, But honestly, would someone complain? How often do you go to someone's house and say, "Seriously, I just need to tell you, what you just served me was disgusting?" Is the fact that no one complained really a measure of a meal?

The horse arrives, cooked. Or "cooked."

Is it well done? Naaaaay. It is practically raw in the middle. So raw that if I sat on the steak and gave a "whoop," it might kick up and take me at a gallop off to the black sand beach of Vík, and canter all the way down to Reynisfjara.

"Is it always cooked this raw?" I ask the waitress, intrepidly.

She laughs. No really, I see she is laughing at me, totally laughing except without the actual laughing part. "Yes," she says.

I eat around the edges. I cannot bring myself to eat the raw parts. There's nothing wrong with it, except that I have Black Beauty galloping through my head, glaring at me with blame and disgust.

Luckily, I'm not very hungry, but all in all it was a very expensive dinner of which I ate very little. Darn the cute front desk guy! I fell prey to his charms and am now out 4800 ISK. I should have gone to a local grocery store instead. At this point, I remember I had planned to borrow a cooler from Mary Frances, so I could bring along my own food and refrigerate what needs refrigerating. Too late now; I'll just have to plan better. No more meals out, or I'll be out of money halfway through my trip.

Throughout my dinner, I notice a fairly constant stream of people coming in to eat, but finding no room. Because I'm seated right near the reception area, I can also hear several people seeking a place to stay for the night, but being turned away. There is no room at the inn, it seems. After dinner I ask Front Desk Guy about this. He says that in summer, it's best to reserve at least a month in advance, if not months. Rooms fill up quickly, he says, and once they're gone, they're gone.

I ask him about Vík. He moved here three years ago. Why? "It's the best place in Iceland," he tells me. The black sand beach in front of you, the glacier behind you, the Northern Lights (late September through early May; you need both cold and dark, he says), everything you could want right near you. It's perfect, he says.

The glacier behind you?

Ah, the disadvantages of bad weather. I had not seen the glacier. Maybe tomorrow.

As for the Hotel Lundi: It is clean, if a bit weary and worn, and it's wonderfully located. As noted in *Pam on the Map: Ireland*, when traveling solo I like to be downtown. Vík is quite small, so "downtown" is relative, I suppose, but I am glad to be within walking distance of everything. The blackout curtains, however, are not so much blackout curtains as they are thick, yellow curtains. They don't make the room dark; they make it yellow. The soap in the shower leaves something to be desired, but I've brought my own. Internet connection is challenging at first, but once I'm in, I'm more or less in. Staff are lovely. Overall, a nice place. I believe the hotel also runs a hostel; I don't have any knowledge of anything hostel-related. After checking in at home and writing a bit, I climb into bed and am quickly asleep.

If I did today again:

Not until after I returned home did I learn about an area called Þórsmörk, a mountain ridge and one of the most popular hiking areas in Iceland. If I'd had it on the itinerary, today would have been the day to do it. Apparently, it is only accessible by specially equipped vehicles, which I am sure my little rental car was not. However, some tour companies offer day trips from Reykjavík to Þórsmörk in the summer. If I go back, I'll definitely look into these options to find out more. If you're a hiker, from what I read it sounds like trails from both Skógafoss and Seljalandsfoss will lead you to the Þórsmörk area.

The Skógar Folk Museum, near Skógafoss, looks like it might be worth a visit, too.

I hear the Seljavallalaug geothermal pool, the first pool built in Iceland, was partially filled with some ash from the Eyjafjallajökull eruption, but apparently is now mostly cleaned up. This pool is "well off the beaten path," but reports say the hike is beautiful, and sitting in the pool surrounded by the spectacular scenery has the potential for bliss. I read in one place that it's only five hundred meters from Seljalandsfoss ... I did see people farther down the trail from where the kids were hiking up the hill? I guess I was that close and didn't even realize it!

Another place I'd like to check out if (when) I come back: the town of Hveragerði, the "Hot Spring Capital of the World," with lots of great hiking trails, hot springs, and a warm river!

Note that access to the cliffs at Dyrhólaey is restricted in May/June for nesting season.

Vík to Hali

Thursday, August 1, 2013

The dawn has broken gloriously. The sun is up, and it is dazzling in its magnificence. And also, I can officially attest to the non-blackoutness of the curtains in the hotel room. In fact, I woke up at 2:30 and the sun was already on the rise, beaming happily through the yellow non-blackout curtains like a premature wake-up call. I tossed a towel over my face to block the light, and went back to sleep until 6:00.

Blackout curtains or no, the day is beautiful, the world is gleaming after yesterday's rain. I'm inspired to take a short morning walk to the beach, to see how things look in the sunlight rather than the fog; to bear witness to this morning's sundrenched world. With fifteen minutes to go before the breakfast room opens at 7:30, I stride down to the black sand beach, admire the serenity of the setting, deeply breathe in the peacefulness of the moment. Another woman is there, sitting purposefully. She may not be in full-on meditation but clearly this is her spot; she has claimed it and I am intruding. I turn around to walk back to the village, and I stop in my tracks, stunned by the beauty before me. Front Desk Guy was right: The glacier is right there, a wide, cool marshmallow-creme-topped backdrop to the town, enormous and dominating and gorgeous. It sits behind the village, watching over it like a cold, omnipresent protector.

Back in the dining room, I peruse the array of food. I suspect one of my choices is herring, but as I haven't seen a lot of herring up close, I'm not quite sure. I'm still traumatized over having eaten Misty of Chincoteague last night, though. I decline what might be herring. Bread, cheese, fruit, juice, a quick goodbye to Front Desk Guy after I find my keys right where they were supposed to be (rather than where I was looking), and I'm off for the day.

Today's eventual destination is Hali, farther east along the southern coast. I'm not entirely sure whether Hali is a town or just the name of the hotel, Hali Country Hotel. On my way out, uncertain whether I'll ever find a gas station again, I gas up. Gas is about 252.9 krona per liter, but I have absolutely no idea what that is in dollars and gallons. It does seem to be consistent station to station within one company, though prices differ from company to company. Here in Vík, I use an N1 station. (I do love very much that my GPS can find gas stations, preprogrammed into the device as "points of interest." Very convenient. Although it would have been basically impossible to miss the station on the way out of Vík.) Being able to actually buy gas has become more important than finding what is cheapest.

It is early morning, by now just a little before 8 a.m., and I am virtually alone on the road. At first this feels luxurious and liberating: I have finally reached the end of the tourist track! Then, as I continue on and the isolation grows deeper, I start to feel slightly anxious: What if I accidentally drive off the road and no one ever,

ever finds me? There are no other cars. I am passing no other cars, and no cars are passing me. I have proven myself not to be the fastest driver in Iceland; I'm still being quite cautious. Already I'm used to other cars coming up on my tail (and they come up very close indeed, those Icelanders, and/or travelers in Iceland!) before whipping around me and racing off into the sun. But here, there is no evidence that I'm not the last driver on Earth. At one point, I go a full thirteen minutes before another car comes at me from the other direction. The solitude is almost eerie.

I am very glad I got gas when I did.

The coastline is far to my right (I am driving the country's Ring Road counterclockwise, in case that isn't obvious), and the aforementioned "shelf" of the previous coastline is high above to my left. As I drive, I bear witness to myriad varieties of barren desolation. Early in today's route the ground is covered in short grassy foliage, waving and rolling in the wind, as far as the eye can see. The landscape of short grass gives way to a vast emptiness sporadically broken up with random rugged mounds of lava rocks, which transforms into low black sandy dunes spotted with tufts of taller grass, which then becomes lumpy lava coated with fire extinguisher green foam, and after that, undulating smooth grassy mounds. All of it low, all of it with an essence of barrenness. It feels untouched. The land is like an adolescent youth, moody, ever changing, undeveloped, uncertain what it wants to be, trying out everything it can think of.

Driving along what was once the bottom of the sea, I can feel the ancient ocean all around me. If I imagine — not closing my eyes, of course; the roads are narrow and require much attention — but if I stop and really imagine it, I can picture myself on the ocean floor, the water level way above my head, mermaids and sea creatures swimming around me, King Neptune floating by, yielding his trident. Surely there's a previously sunken treasure some-where, uncovered here in this barrenness, waiting for me? I can see for miles in all directions. If there's something out there, I'd see it. Unless the elves are hiding it. Which they might be.

The landscape gives a mind a lot of time to wander.

When I reach a turnoff, I pull off to the right a bit and stop to take a video of the area. It's hard to adequately describe the vast-ness and magnificence and spacious immensity of the Icelandic landscape, and equally difficult to capture it in pictures. Even pan-oramic pictures don't give you the full sense of the enormity of the land, how far you can see, how open and empty it is. In places like this, Iceland feels endless and desolate.

Later, the landscape is completely barren — so barren that by the way the car is handling itself, I think it's quite windy outside, but there isn't a blade of glass against which to confirm my theory. And then, eventually, there is grass again, a tuft here, a tuft there, then larger patches again, enough to support occasional wildlife. I see sheep off the side of the road. One sheep jumps and runs, sud-denly, joyfully. I imagine the sheep crying out to the other sheep, "Look! It's grass! There's grass over here! Oh my gosh, grass! This is awesome!" before bounding over and munching away on the green delight.

It is windy here.

At one point, I am driving along and I see ahead of me a gush-ing tornado of dirt, racing straight across the road in the wind, from my left to my right, from the other side of the road to mine and then back into the open desert. I am going to have to drive through it. The road is just as narrow here as anywhere; there is hardly any shoulder and there is no room for error. For a good while now I've felt the wind tugging at my tiny car, a subcompact Suzuki Swift, trying to toss it off the pavement. I am already steer-ing into the center of the road, taking my half out of the middle (as my family would have said of my great-grandfather's driving), in an effort to ensure I don't get blown off the side.

I grip the wheel and drive through. It's only about twenty road feet of whirling dust in the wind, but it is enough to get my adrenaline pumping. Once I'm through, I take some deep breaths and drive on in the nothingness.

Now. Let's take a moment to discuss bathrooms.

As I see it, and with all the driving I have had some time to think about this, there are two primary challenges to traveling Iceland's Ring Road. Well, two and a half; the first one and a half are related.

1. You can't possibly stop to see everything you want to see (and take pictures of), because if you do, you'll be stopping non-stop. (Haha, get it? Stopping non-stop?)

   1a. Even if you could stop to see everything you wanted to see, you couldn't stop to see everything you wanted to see because the roads have NO SHOULDERS and you can't pull over for about ninety-five percent of the road, without falling off the road. So if you see something gorgeous, which you will, just soak it in with your eyes. Unless you're driving, then just glance really quickly or you'll drive off the road because again, NO SHOULDERS.

2. Not only does the Ring Road have no shoulders, it also has no bathrooms.

When I say no bathrooms, I mean no bathrooms. No toilets. No place to see a man about a horse. (Figuratively, that is. Literally, there are lots of places to see a man about a horse. See previous discussion of horse farms.)

So, let's say you're driving along and you've been drinking your recommended amount of water for the day and suddenly you think, "I need to see a man about a horse," and you mean it figuratively, and you REALLY need to see a man about a horse, but there's nowhere to pull over.

Not only that, but even if you did pull over, there are no trees. And no bushes. Nothing to hide behind and then come back out from with a look on your face like, "What? I wasn't doing anything back there. It was just a really interesting-looking bush and I wanted to see the other side of it, with my pants down." If you did pull over, if you're lucky you're a guy and you could just turn the other way, but then people coming the other way would see you; there's no escaping it. But if you're a woman, unless you have one of those stand-to-pee things (do people actually use those things? Because (1) awkward, and (2) what do you do with it after you've used it? Because I do not want that in my purse.) … where was I … unless you have one of those stand-to-pee things, you now have your pants down and your behind is hanging out on the side of the road in Iceland where not only can drivers passing by see you, but because it's all flat and you can see for MILES, that means anyone who might be miles away taking a picture of a glacier with a telephoto lens or something could also see you carefully balanced in a bare-bummed squat, and you could end up in that picture, and then when that person got home from their trip, their friends would laugh at you photobombing (or would that be photobumming?) the glacier picture with your naked ass. And then it would end up online, and even if they put a black bar over your eyes to keep your identity private, your friends would know that (1) you were in Iceland, and (2) those are your clothes, so (3) that bare behind is yours. And then you'd have to quit your job and move to a new state and, depending on how serious it was, register with the witness protection program, all because you had to pee at an inopportune time in Iceland.

I'm not kidding about this, either. While I haven't witnessed any women peeing in the non-woods in Iceland, I have witnessed two men and a boy peeing into the wind, in three days on the road.

For those just joining us, that's an average of one a day, which is on average about one a day more than I see in my day-to-day life on the road at home. Granted I've been on the road a lot the last three days. Still, it is a high average. And if I've seen three males peeing in the limited number of locations I've visited so far in Iceland, then chances are there are men and boys ALL OVER ICELAND, peeing on the side of the road.

So. Iceland Tourism: Bathrooms, please. Or at least plant an occasional bush and build up a shoulder on the road by the bush so someone can pull over to use the bush. Is that too much to ask?

All right, then.

So, the first stop of the day is Kirkjugólf. Back home, when I was researching online, I occasionally had a hard time finding places in Iceland. But I imagined that once I got here, the local GPS would know everything, right?

Not so. Again.

My GPS does not know Kirkjugólf. My GPS mocks me, in fact, for not having written down anything but "Kirkjugólf." I know what this place is, though; it's a place where there are more hexagonal basalt columns, like at Reynisfjara, except here they are on the ground. Normally, as at Reynisfjara, you see the columns from the side, but in this place they are like a tiled floor. You can stand on top of them (Kirkjugólf, in fact, means "church floor"). I am determined that I will find this.

I type "Kirk" into the GPS to see what it might suggest. (I briefly think that if I named my GPS, if we had a better relationship, it might be more accommodating. But I am too busy finding Kirkjugólf to come up with a name right now. Work with me, GPS!)

The GPS offers up Kirkjubæjarklaustur, and I think, yes, that's right, that sounds familiar. That's something I've heard of. From the bearing — it's to the east of where I am — that sounds correct.

I click "Go!" for Kirkjubæjarklaustur, and eventually, after all the open emptiness, I arrive at this small village, population just over one hundred. Note that there is nothing — nothing — between Vík and Kirkjubæjarklaustur. Bring water, gas up the car, bring food. (There is, of course, no bathroom along the route. Don't go too crazy with the water.) Finally, at Kirkjubæjarklaustur you can fuel up again, both you and your car.

But my car and I are doing just fine and don't need fuel. Instead, I look along the road for some signs to Kirkjugólf, now that I'm in the general area. Eventually I see a giant directional sign and map, which looks promising. I pull over and get out. Another family is there, and together, an older gentleman in broken English and me in mine, swatting away dozens of tiny flying midges that are attracted to our carbon dioxide and our heat, we agree on a route — down the road to the left just a ways.

The "church floor" is very close to the directional sign, in fact; we could have walked to it. But we drive the half mile or so, pull in, and walk over to the tiles. I'm not sure what I was expecting, but it seems almost anticlimactic. Maybe because they're so out in the open. I don't know why that surprises me, but it does. This tiled floor is just exposed rock in a field of short grass.

I step on top of the hexagonal tiles, and imagine the columns extending below my feet to the center of the Earth. The setting could not be more stunning. Tucked in under the old coastline shelf, with bright blue sky above and grassy farmland all around, Kirkjubæjarklaustur seems like a lovely place in which to make a life. Strange that it's so far from everything else.

If I haven't seen enough of my beloved hexagonal columns, next is Svartifoss, or "black falls," a waterfall in Vatnajökull National Park. It is so named because of the dark lava columns over which it cascades on its way down to its base. They're the same columns you see everywhere, but at this particular site for some reason they're just a bit darker, it seems.

Vatnajökull National Park is another area where a person could spend days just wandering; Vatnajökull is the largest and most voluminous of Iceland's glaciers, and is one of Europe's biggest. When I reach the Skaftafell visitor centre, it's clear that it is a hub from which countless adventures begin. The parking lot is full of cars, tour buses, camper vans, people coming and going with walking sticks and backpacks and maps. The visitor centre itself has a store filled with books, toys, postcards, CDs, DVDs, maps, and tempting souvenirs of all types. If I were the shopping type, I'd be able to tell you more about what was there. Undoubtedly shot glasses and scarves and beer mugs and keychains, all the usuals. As far as my needs, though, all I need is a postcard to send home to my niece and nephew, and a stamp to get it there. I engage in a brief postcard-rack-turning dance with another traveler looking at the same cards, pick out one of Svartifoss on a sunny day, and ask at the counter about stamps. May I buy them here? Yes I may. How much to send a postcard to the U.S.? Well, it's by grams. This is in the 50g-and-under category, so it's 230 ISK. I calculate roughly in my head. I think that's around $2? Maybe? A lot for postage, it seems. Still, my niece and nephew are worth $2, plus the price of the postcard. All in all I spend about $6 for that postcard. It had better arrive on time and gilded around the edges.

I find a flat surface outside on which to write out a quick message to the kiddos, and drop the postcard in the mail. Incidentally, if you're looking for the Icelandic post, the logo is red and white and looks like a misshapen tree. On closer inspection you will see it is not a tree, but rather a "P" for "Pósturinn," with a simplified horn behind it. (Remembering my Icelandic lessons from Car Rental Guy, I think that is "Póstur," or "Post," and the "inn" part indicates it is THE Post. I'm just guessing here, but it sounds like a good story, so I'm sticking to it.) I drop it in the Pósturinn box, and head off to find Svartifoss.

Getting to this waterfall takes a bit more of a hike than I've had so far. I've read that there are a few different starting points for trails to the falls: a mostly easy but much longer trail from the visitor centre, a shorter trail but with a much more difficult start from another parking lot a little farther along, and a fairly easy trail only open to tour buses in summer. Thinking I'll save myself some time, I drive to the second parking lot and head out. It is, in fact, quite strenuous at the start, very steep for the first bit, but eventually I am triumphant over the climb. I regain my ability to breathe, pass by a couple other falls, and finally reach the first real viewpoint from which you get a good view of Svartifoss. You can get closer, walk down right to the base of the waterfall, it seems, but the previous climb was enough for this gal for the day, so I utilize the "zoom" feature on my camera to trick people into thinking I walked all the way in. Shh, don't tell anyone.

Something about the hexagonal columns at Svartifoss makes this waterfall look like it is springing forth from a giant pipe organ on the side of the cliff, made up of hundreds or thousands of pipes, covered in a rich black/brown patina farther up the falls and a softer, lighter brown down below. Or, because the columns on top have broken off from below, if you squint and use your imagination it looks a bit like a shawl made up of pillars of lava columns, draped around the shoulders of the waterfall. It is not a particularly voluminous waterfall, especially after Gullfoss, Skógafoss, or even Seljalandsfoss, but the setting is spectacular. I can see Vatnajökull ("Glacier of Rivers") peering out from behind the hill I'm standing on; the slight chill in the air declares its presence as well.

I hike back to my car, checking its tires when I get there. With the memory of those cars I saw on my first day here, driving with flat tires and nary a soul around to care, I've remained paranoid and have an impending sense of doom about my own car's tires. I am sure something is going to happen with one of the tires. This results in an endless loop of, "Now that I've thought something will happen to the tires, something will happen to the tires," and I can't win. As a result, I check the tires every time I get in and out of the car. So far, so good. Fingers crossed.

Next on the list, Jökulsárlón. This is a large glacial lake on the outskirts of Vatnajökull National Park; the icebergs in Jökulsárlón have broken off Vatnajökull's glaciers. I've read accounts from visitors to Iceland that Jökulsárlón was the highlight of their trips, so naturally I'm skeptical. I don't want to set expectations too high, or I'll be disappointed. Besides which, it's just ice floating in water. How spectacular can that be?

When I glimpse Jökulsárlón for the first time, I literally gasp out loud.

I could not be here on a more perfect day. The sun is out in full force, the sky is blue, the clouds are white, the glacier dazzles in majestic magnificence. And the lake, the lake is an impossible, deep, rich turquoise blue, clear and crisp; it sends chills through my spine just from the sight of it. The icebergs range in size, some slabs look to be bigger than houses, bigger than an apartment complex. The tiniest icebergs, nearly melted, the size of a fist, a finger. Most are the white of the clouds. Some have thick black lines through them: the result of ashfall? Evidence of Eyjafjallajökull's eruption — or even the eruption of another volcano, many years prior? I am in awe.

I pull in to a parking lot where a woman is handing full-body suits to groups of people; more suits hang on a standing rack to the side. A couple companies offer boat trips through the lagoon, and I'm assuming the suits are to keep you warm while you're on board. I've been standing outside for a only few minutes and already I'm zipping up my jacket and tightening my hood around my face. The chill is immediate, insistent, penetrating. So far on my trip, the weather has been mild and pleasant, but here I find myself thinking longingly of gloves and a warm scarf.

But I'm in no hurry. This sight is magical. I don't know how it would be in the rain; cold and miserable and magnificent and beautiful? But in this sunshine, the panorama is breathtaking, extraordinary.

Off to the left I notice a trail. Leaving no trail unfollowed, I explore to see where it goes. Turns out it's the path down to the dock from which the Zodiac boats launch. A group has just disembarked and is coming up the trail, faces red from the wind and the cold, but with shining eyes and bright smiles, enraptured by the magic of the icy lagoon. Something about this place inspires wonder. I don't know if the wind carries away the voices or if I'm so mesmerized by the sight that I don't hear them, but there's an intense serenity to Jökulsárlón. I watch icebergs float along the river, some slowly, some quickly, and I imagine if it weren't for the cold I could stare for hours. Watching the ghostly chunks of ice drift in the vivid blue of the water is hypnotizing. But the cold is biting. I decide against a boat trip; I can only imagine how chilly it would be, though I'm sure the up-close views of the glaciers would be thrilling.

I can see another viewpoint, across the river, buzzing with more people. I hop in my car, drive across the Glacier River Bridge, turn left into the parking area, and find rock star parking up at the front row. This is somewhat amazing; every site I've been to seems to be at full capacity, with almost exactly the same number of cars as possible parking spots. Either someone has planned the attractions with extreme in-and-out volume precision, or these sites can't take much more traffic than they currently get, unless someone expands the parking areas.

I and my camera get out of the car again, and I wander, staring, taking it all in. From this viewpoint I get a more expansive view of lagoon, glacier, and the full landscape. I can't tear my eyes away, and spend a long time meandering up and down the shore and hills, just breathing in the cool air, listening to the wind-muted cacophony of the sea birds (mostly arctic terns), watching the play of the sunlight on the water and the way the sunbeams become shimmering, dancing diamonds when they hit the surface of the lagoon, and admiring the confident, timeless splendor of the glacier.

But eventually, it's time to go. Last stop, my next hotel. On my way out of the parking lot, I see two handsome, jovial men, probably in their late twenties or early thirties, laughing by the side of the road as they try to hitch a ride. They look so friendly and jubilant that I'm tempted; surely they're harmless (and definitely they're handsome, probably even more so after a good shower). I'm almost certain they're harmless, in fact, but the "almost" isn't good enough. I smile and wave at them and drive on. I've noticed a good number of hitchhikers here, actually, and every time, I'm tempted to pick them up. Iceland feels safe like that: Other places may have axe murderers and psychopaths, but certainly people needing rides in Iceland are all jolly and entertaining, right? Probably so. Probably so. But the uncertainty wins out.

My hotel is the Hali Country Hotel, which I think is in Hali, but GPS does not have any idea where "Hali" is. On the one hand, I imagine if I keep driving the Ring Road, I'll get there; supposedly it's not that far. On the other hand, I don't want to miss it. There might not be another hotel for hours, and from what I've experienced, even if there is, it will be full. I look at my itinerary and see "Suðursveit" is also part of the address. My GPS refuses to acknowledge this word. There are two more words listed on my itinerary in conjunction with this hotel, Sveitarfélagið and Hornafjörður. Magically, the GPS gives Hornafjörður its blessing, and I can now type in the street name and number. I head on; it's just after 5 p.m. and the everlasting sunset is not even beginning to fall behind me in the west.

Shortly after 5:15 I arrive, and on seeing the hotel I remember part of why I chose it: The side is decorated to look like a line of giant books. The hotel is also home to a cultural center, with an exhibition dedicated to Icelandic author Þórbergur Þórðarson (1888-1974), who grew up in the area.

On talking with the woman at the cashier area (which seems to cover the restaurant, store, and possibly the museum as well), I learn two things: (1) people in Iceland can buy ebooks (but not print books) from Amazon.com (which answers for me the question of whether my books are available to the people of this lovely country); and (2) there are no other restaurants or food sources within a forty-five-minute drive. I chide myself for forgetting to always plan ahead and find food at grocery stores when I could. Now I'm stuck at this hotel, with no real choice but to partake of the rather expensive one-price-fits-all buffet dinner. The website says "reasonable price," but at 5200 ISK — just under $45 — this seems exorbitant to me, especially as I'm not particularly hungry and won't get my full value out of the buffet. This trip is already quite costly, and eating budget meals was one way I was going to scrape some pennies off the expense. But, seeing as my choice is to drive an hour to Höfn (and back), with the associated high cost of gas, buffet dinner it is.

My room, in another building closer to the ocean, is fabulous. There's a sign at the entrance asking people to remove their shoes, to preserve the spotless hardwood floors; this seems a bit unrealistic, I'd say, and I just walk carefully to my room and take off my shoes once inside. The room is spacious and clean, with a wonderful view of the interior coastline shelf (rooms on the opposite side of the hall look out over the Atlantic Ocean). I tap into the hotel WiFi, send some messages home, then head to the buffet. This B&B is completely full too, just as Hotel Lundi was last night. Booking well in advance in summer in Iceland seems like a very good idea.

Dinner is delicious. The restaurant raises its own tasty arctic char (trout), and I also sample lamb in a couple different forms. (I keep hoping for someone to serve reindeer, but I haven't seen any yet. Is that so wrong? If I can eat Black Beauty then surely I can eat Rudolph.) Very soon, I'm full. I head back to my gorgeous room, write, read a bit from Game of Thrones, but start dozing off quickly. I close the luxuriously thick blackout curtains — these, I can tell, will do their job — and go to bed.

Next time I'm in the area:

When I was researching Iceland, I read about something called "The Enchanted Realm." As far as I can tell, this is another name for the Skaftafell ice caves. They look gorgeous — caves of ice! — but would take some time and effort, and you'd need to go with a guide for certain. And, I'm not entirely sure these adventures are available in summer; it may be a winter thing. These caves were recently mentioned in a BBC "Earth's most otherworldly places" list. I'd say they'd be worth a look.

The beautiful area of Landmannalaugar would actually be a stop for either yesterday's or today's itinerary — it's basically north of Vík. Descriptions of the landscape make it sound spectacular, multicolored rhyolite mountains with hues of pink, brown, green, yellow, blue, purple, black, and white. You can't go there with a 2WD car, however. Daily bus tours will take you out to Landmannnalaugar from Reykjavík, mid-June through mid-September, or you can also get tours from Skaftafell. You can stop in the area for a couple hours, or I'm guessing you could make reservations at the Landmannalaugar Hut and stay overnight, heading back out on the next day's bus.

As I mentioned, you could spend days in Vatnajökull National Park if you like camping and/or hiking. The area is one of Iceland's many true gems.

Fjaðrárgljúfur Canyon: This canyon looks spectacular in the pictures I saw online; however, it's off a 2WD-rental-car-verboten "F" road, so you have to have 4WD to get yourself there. According to the directions I found online, a little before Kirkjubæjarklaustur (when heading east) you exit left (north) onto F206 toward Lakagígjar. After few minutes the road to Laki heads off to the right; stay straight instead and in a few minutes you'll get to Fjaðrárgljúfur. F206 is on the Big Map I got from Car Rental Guy, but when I search online maps, F206 doesn't even show up. I'm guessing that means it's a pretty rough road. If you go, send me pictures!

If you have more time to spend in the area, check out the tours to Cape Ingólfshöfði. The cape is about halfway between Skaftafell and Jökulsárlón and is home to thousands of nesting seabirds. I've read that there's a tour that will take you there in a tractor-drawn hay cart. Sounds like fun — especially if you dress warmly!

Hali to Akureyri

Friday, August 2, 2013

Buckle up, people. Today, we drive.

When I was planning this trip, I came across a logistical co-nundrum. I wanted to see the south, at least out to Jökulsárlón. I wanted to see the city of Akureyri and the north. I wanted to rent a car. I had obligations keeping me in Reykjavík on certain days. I could rent a car, drive to Jökulsárlón and back to Reykjavík, then fly out to Akureyri and rent another car and drive the "Diamond Circle" around the northern sites, and return the car to Akureyri and fly back. And at some point I could also take the rented car from Reykjavík and drive out to the Snæfellsnes peninsula, and … well, it all got very convoluted, and there was a lot of backtracking (which I hate), and the expense of renting two cars for only a few days each, plus a round trip flight to Akureyri.…

And so, ultimately, I decided to rent one car, eschew all flights within the country, and drive the arc of Iceland around the east coast. After all, I want to see the whole country, right? Visit all the places! See all the things! Not just the popular bits and the well traveled routes, but the whole shebang.

And then at some point, for some reason, I decided I would drive the whole east coast in one day. I'm not entirely sure why. In my research I didn't find much I wanted to see on the east coast, I suppose, and I hate to "waste time." Of all the things that bug me, wasting time is high on the list. I already have far too little time in this country. I can drive all day, I figured, get that bit over with, and then get on with Akureyri and the north.

So today, we drive. A lot.

When I mapped out the route online, the map site told me this drive will take just under seven hours. That's without stopping. I have very few stops planned, so I'm sure the actual drive will only take about seven hours. Right? What could go wrong?

I've told the Hali Country Hotel I want to leave early. Cashier Woman very kindly, without my requesting it, passed on to the breakfast staff that I'd love to start breakfast at 7:00, rather than 7:30 when the restaurant usually opens. I told her it wasn't necessary, but she's already done it, so at 7:00, my car is packed, I've left my beautiful, serene, writer's-retreat kind of room, and am scoping out the breakfast goods the staff have just begun to set out.

Shortly after I sit down with some Skyr (yogurt), eggs, fruit, and tea, a couple comes in. I saw them at dinner last night, heard them speaking English with a thick accent I couldn't identify. I say hello, ask where they're from. Switzerland! I don't know if you know this, but I am 7/8 Swiss (and 1/8 Dutch). My family took a trip to Switzerland in 2007 (you can even read about it in my short retrospective *Pam on the Map: Switzerland* book), and it's one of my favorite countries so far. This couple is from near Zürich. True Swiss, they love to hike and had originally contemplated walking around Iceland, but decided it looked a bit rough, with the unpredictable weather and challenging roads and whatnot. So they've been driving around for a week, and have another week to go.

Then another couple comes in (it is still before the appointed 7:30 breakfast time, and I wonder whether they all told Cashier Woman they wanted early breakfasts too). They are also from Switzerland. This couple is from near Lucerne. They've been doing Iceland in a big figure-8, visiting the Reykjavík area, Snæfellsnes, and the Westfjords, before crossing over the highlands to do the southern portion. They tell me they visited Svartifoss a few days ago; I comment that it was quite a hike to the top. The woman smiles, says it was "just a stroll." I recount to her the tale of my family's hike from Kleine Scheidegg to Männlichen in Switzerland, a hike my dad had deemed "all uphill," but on which we saw nuns meandering along carrying their purses. (Granted, they were going in the other direction, which would make it "all downhill," but still.) The woman laughs and says yes, Kleine Scheidegg to Männlichen is "just a Sunday stroll" to the Swiss. Here in Iceland, they are taking every chance they get to explore on foot, she tells me. She nods at her husband and says, "He doesn't like it if he can't hike." Today, they'll be off on a bird watching tour, returning to Hali in the evening.

I take a bit of pride in knowing we Swiss are all up early, taking on the day, not burning daylight. I suppose, since the sun was up hours before us (if it even ever went down; I haven't seen true darkness since I've been here), technically we have burned daylight. But that Swiss temperament, efficient, making good use of time: Yes! Iceland is still asleep but we Swiss are up and ready. I give cheerful goodbyes to my fellow Swiss people, wish them all well, and am on my way.

Iceland really is asleep in the early morning hours. That's not entirely true, of course. The staff were all up, hard at work making breakfast for us; other people around the country are undoubtedly taking showers and having coffee and reading the morning paper before heading off to their jobs. But the country feels so calm and serene and undisturbed. That feeling I had when I was driving yesterday morning, the ominous feeling of isolation, of being the last person in the world, I now suspect the lack of traffic was also due to the early hour. As I turn east back onto the Ring Road, two sheep who have spent the night at the base of the Hali directional sign gaze up at me sleepily but somehow grumpily, like teenagers who didn't want to be awakened just yet.

And, in fact, I find there are sheep all over the road this early in the morning. Sleeping on it, jumping across it, wandering down the center of it, leaving deposits on it. I frequently have to slow down and adjust my speed. The sheep, well, I don't want to say they're not smart; they just have different brains than humans, you know? And their brains don't tell them, "Hey, a car is coming, get out of the road." Their brains seem to tell them, "Hey, there's something on the road, probably dangerous, so think for a bit about what you want to do about it. See where the other sheep go first. Don't rush into any decisions. You don't want to be on this side of the road when all the other sheep are on that side." Only they're probably thinking it in Sheep Icelandic, I'm assuming.

Despite the sheep, or maybe in part because of it, I am in love with driving in Iceland in the morning. It feels like I have the country all to myself.

My first, very brief stop is to gas up at Höfn, which I am told is pronounced "Hup," and I have a hard time believing this but I've heard it from several sources, so it must be true? Driving into town I see tents and camper vans lined up all along a grassy area. A truck ahead of me carrying some sort of motorcycle-like vehicle turns into the designated parking area, at which time I see signs that indicate there's a motocross rally in town this weekend. I'm reminded with retrospective fondness of a motorcycle rally I went to with friends in Ireland. I say "retrospective" fondness because the music was ear-splitting loud all night, and I "slept" with my ears plugged, but it made a good story afterwards! The Höfn gas station is open, and I do my "I don't have a chip-and-PIN card, can I pay in here?" routine, get gas, and head back out past the motocross crowd, as they slowly wake up for their big day.

As expected, the first part of the drive takes me through wide open spaces, past lots of sheep enjoying breakfast and telling each other about whatever crazy sheep dreams they had last night, how they had to count people to help themselves get to sleep, whatever sheep talk about in the morning, and not a whole lot else. There seem to be fewer houses tucked into the land at the bottom of the cliff out this way; fewer people, fewer everything.

I've heard people sometimes refer to the Icelandic landscape as "otherworldly" or a "moonscape." I disagree with this description. It's not otherworldly; it's very much of this world. It's just a much younger version of this world. I look at the Icelandic landscape and feel like I can see back in time, how the Earth, the parts of it we're familiar with, morphed and changed itself through the ages. Before the dirt had all built up. Before everything was tamed. Wild and barren, but yet varied and vivid and burgeoning with possibility.

To pass the time, I count the minutes between the cars coming at me from the other direction. About one car per minute, in this first part of the drive. The roads are still narrow, but there's no one else on them.

Except when there are tour buses.

By 8:30 a.m., I've passed three full-size buses. Each time, I grab the wheel and hold tight. The buses are nearly the width of their lane, and there's not much room for error on either side. I've heard there are reindeer out this way, and I see one, off to the right! But just as I see it, the third of the tour buses looms ahead, bearing down on me with the swift and steady confidence of a driver who knows the roads, knows his vehicle is bigger than mine, and has places he has to be. I can't let my gaze wander. I glance quickly at the reindeer (sitting, or kneeling; it too is not yet fully awake), then whip past. Hopefully I'll see more reindeer. I still haven't seen one puffin. Mostly, it's sheep and horses, sheep and horses, sheep and horses.

Somewhere past Höfn, I reach a tunnel, the Almannaskarðs-göng, cutting through the side of the mountain and under a pass. I don't know about you, but when I get to a tunnel, I think, "Oh, cool! A tunnel! This is awesome!" because passing through a tunnel in a mountain, that's awesome!

In theory, that is. Because in reality, it's a tunnel. Once in the tunnel, of course I can't see anything but the tunnel. My GPS tells me it can't find a signal and is going to go off to get a snack and find a toilet. Maybe that's just me, fantasizing about a snack and a toilet. At any rate, the GPS goes dark. The tunnel stretches for about a mile, and then I'm back out in the light. I am still alone in the world.

Eventually, the landscape changes completely, and there is no green to be seen anywhere. The road cuts right into the edge of the hillside, which spills straight into the ocean. Unlike previously, when the old coastline shelf paralleled my drive several miles in from the shore, now I'm driving along on the very edge of the country. I can see why this particular area is not teeming with visitors. There is nothing here.

A while later, I'm at a fjord, at least I think it's a fjord, and there are signs of life again. I pass a gang of swans, which of course makes me think of Björk, the Icelandic singer who for a very long time was all I knew of Iceland, and the swan dress she wore years ago. I think about what a group of swans must be called. Probably not a gang. Probably something fancier and nicer. A pirouette of swans. A treasure of swans.

I pass the swans.

And then comes gravel road. This is okay; I've heard not all of the Ring Road is paved, so I'm prepared. But then! Shortly after I hit the gravel road, my GPS wants me to turn off the main road. I thought I was taking Highway 1 the whole way around? I pull off the road as best I can (no cars around anyway), and look in confusion at the road signs. The road leading off straight ahead has a 1 in a solid box. The road the GPS wants to send me down, off to the left, has a 1 in a dotted box. There is gravel road in both directions. Why does my GPS want to send me off on a 1 with a dotted box? I pull out one of the maps I bought while waiting at the airport for Car Rental Guy to show up, and ponder and peruse. I quickly see that the dotted-1 road, the 939, is a much shorter route. A shortcut leading back to Highway 1, solid-box 1, after a few miles. And at this point both routes are gravel, so what do I have to lose? Shorter sounds good to me. I head up the 939.

Within five minutes, I regret it.

This road! Why the heck did my GPS send me on this road? What have I ever done to my GPS to make it hate me so? This road is not only gravel, but loose gravel, with a steep grade. It's narrow enough that in most places two cars cannot safely pass, and it creeps and curls around curves on the mountain I'm apparently now climbing over. I grit my teeth and wrap my hands tightly around the wheel and hope fervently that no cars come from the other direction, because if they do, I haven't a clue what will happen. I can't back up and I'm sure the other person wouldn't be able to either. On my left is a sheer drop off into I don't even know what, because I keep repeating to myself, over and over and out loud,

"Don't look. Don't look. Don't look." I just keep my eyes on the road and hope the tires don't lose their grip on the road, sending me plummeting backwards to my death; or that no one comes careening around a corner, hitting me and sending me plummeting to my death, or that I don't overcompensate for the slipping tires and hit the gas too hard and drive forward off the cliff, plummeting to my death. It's a theme. Not wanting to die.

"Don't look. Don't look." Not, "Don't look down," but just don't look anywhere other than this brown gravel/dirt road, up which I am driving at about 10 mph, heart in my throat, eyes on the road.

The road seems to go on forever. I feel my hands sweating; my breathing is shallow, and while I while I wouldn't say I'm scared, I also wouldn't say I'm not. I want off this road. I want to go back and take the other road, which can't possibly be worse, no matter what, it just can't possibly be worse. This road goes on and on, up and up, endlessly, and my only choice is to keep driving. And then, eventually, I can see I'm almost at the top. I can see that there isn't much more hill to the hill, so I must be near the middle, if not the end. I feel this elation. I made it! I didn't die! I didn't plummet to my death! I have survived!

At the top of the pass, there's a wide open space off to the left where I can pull in for a pause. I park, peel my hands off the wheel, peel my behind from the seat, and get out of the car into the fresh air. There's a waterfall here, of course; there are waterfalls everywhere. This one, though, feels like it was placed here just for me, a reward for having made it to the top of the hill without dying. Two sheep are lounging by the side of the waterfall, watching me. They seem somewhat surprised to see me here. I imagine (probably incorrectly) that these sheep don't get much action in these parts. I might be the first human they've ever seen! Because I did not, in fact, run into any other cars en route, neither coming up behind me nor coming the other way. Maybe no one has driven this road since it was first built!

The sheep watch me, unimpressed with my triumph. "We climb mountains like that every day, lady," they seem to be thinking. "It's not such a big deal, pitiful human."

Four years ago when I went to Scotland with my sister and cousin, we drove one particularly precarious road up and over a mountainside, from Applecross to Tornapress. It wasn't as hair-raising as this road, but I did have the same "Don't look down" mantra when I drove it. At the midpoint of that road, there was a similar open spot where people could pull over, park, take a break from the driving, and rest. There was a tradition of rock stacking at that pull-out; from what I could tell, hundreds of previous passersby had stopped and made little rock stacks to mark their success in having driven the route, before continuing on their way.

I decide to do the same here. I find three small rocks and stack them. I watch the waterfall for a few minutes, stare at the sheep, get back in my car, and continue on. No time for celebration. There is, after all, much more road to be driven, and I don't know what's ahead.

The road is not so bad after the midpoint, and I do eventually see cars again on the gravel route. There's a point where the actual Highway 1 (solid-box 1) meets up with this gravel road I'm on, before the road returns to its lovely paved self again. I suspect the cars I met coming the other way were continuing on the long way around. I'm sure the 939 is some people's idea of a great time, but it is not mine.

I drive on. Next stop, then: the Lagarfljót Worm. Iceland's equivalent of the Loch Ness Monster.

As perhaps one might imagine, I have not devoted a lot of time to this stop. The story of the Lagarfljót Worm is that a woman gave her daughter a gold ring, and the daughter wanted to know how to make the most money from it. The mother told her to put the ring under a small lingworm or "heath dragon." Problem is, the dragon grew really big really fast, so the girl tossed the ring and the dragon into the lake, where it grew to the proportions we find at it today, around about a football field long. It's "serpentine," or many-humped, unlike ol' Loch Ness, which is said to be one-humped. And the thing is, some people say that sightings of it (which have been ongoing since 1345) portend natural disaster. (Perhaps such as the Laki eruption of 1783-84, an event in south Iceland during which lava flows and explosions lasted for eight months. EIGHT MONTHS. Look it up. Also known as the "Skaftár Fires." Interesting stuff.) Thinking of the recent volcanic eruption that brought flights to a standstill worldwide, I'd rather not see The Worm and then bring mass destruction to the world. I'm thoughtful like that.

Besides which, when we went to Scotland, we went on a Loch Ness Monster cruise. This may come as no surprise to some, but we didn't see the monster. A part of me is starting to suspect these monsters might not actually exist.

Regardless, the Lagarfljót Worm and Lake Lagarfljót are on my route. The town of Egilsstaðir, where I'll be stopping to get gas and lunch, is at one end of the lake, and is right on the Ring Road. If I happen to see The Worm there, all's the better. (Unless, of course, as discussed, it leads to natural disaster.)

Along the way, I contemplate a few observations about driving around Iceland:

1. Picnics. On occasion you'll see the old familiar "picnic" sign, indicating that there's a spot coming up where you can pull over. At these places there's generally at least a picnic table at which you can sit and enjoy the scenery and eat the food you have in the cooler you remembered to pack, because you're smart like that. However, the sign for picnic spot is a picnic ta-

ble with a tree next to it. Ninety percent of the time (or more), I guarantee you there's no actual tree.

2. The narrow roads, and the fact that the majority of bridges I am driving over seem to be one-lane bridges. You have to keep your eyes open (this is not too difficult; there's not much traffic and you can usually see a good ways ahead), and then if a person coming the other direction gets to the bridge first, they have the right of way. You stop and wait for them to cross, and then it's your turn.

But honestly, is it really necessary to have built only one lane? Really?

I find myself imagining a conversation between officials in Icelandic Government and Road Issues (not a real department):

Government Official 1: "Do you know, I think our roads are very narrow. Maybe we should build wider roads? And what of all these one-lane bridges? Why do we put in only one lane? While we are building, should we not put in two lanes?"

Government Official 2: "You are crazy. This is crazy talk. Narrow roads demand the people's attention. If you start widening the roads, people will get lazy. Then the next thing you know they will be demanding rest stops along the route so they don't have to pee on the side of the road. Narrow roads and holding one's pee, these things build character. We are a nation of characters. End of discussion."

I suppose, when you are only passing one car per minute, it makes sense not to build wide roads. There's not a lot of competition for the road. Still, the edges of the lane, so close to the edge of the road, continue to make me nervous.

Eventually, I make it to Egilsstaðir. A huge town! Compared to everything I've seen the last few days, Egilsstaðir, with its 2,300 people, feels enormous. There are multiple roads! And more than one gas station! And what looks like a warehouse grocery store! Incidentally, Magnús Ver Magnússon, who four times won the World's Strongest Man competition, hails from Egilsstaðir. I tried to contact him for an interview, but alas, no luck. My visit to Iceland will be World's Strongest Man free. The country seems to have a knack for winning the title though. I have no idea why. Iceland has won eight gold medals in the competition, second only to the U.S's nine. Any Icelander will tell you that if you measure gold medals per capita, this is a slam dunk win for Iceland. (Not to mix sports analogies. Is there slam dunking in the World's Strongest Man competition?) Maybe there are so many winners because people have to lift cars out of the ditch after they drove off the narrow roads?

Or not.

I steer toward the grocery store, a Bónus. A tour bus is sitting in the lot. As I enter the store, the sheer number of people in the entryway, along with the general chaos, suggests to me that they arrived on that very tour bus only a few minutes before me. Aside from my quick stop on my way out of Reykjavík, this is my first visit to a full store, so I meander a bit to get my bearings. I am intrigued to find that rather than having refrigerator cases, there's a whole cold room, within which all the goods just sit on normal shelves. You walk in, get cold, get your stuff, get out. Efficient, I suppose? It must be, or they wouldn't do it that way?

I also notice that, as one might expect, all the writing is in Icelandic. I've had such an easy time so far, with everyone speaking English fluently, that it sort of slipped my mind that of course all the food would be labeled in Icelandic. There's a similarity to German (the language I "learned" in high school) in some Icelandic words; for example, potato is Kartoffel in German and kartafla in Icelandic. This, combined with visual cues, suggests to me that kartöflusalat is potato salad. But there is much I can't translate, and frankly, I'm quite wary of the fermented (or "putrefied," which sounds far worse) shark I've heard mentioned so often. I realize that normal Icelanders probably don't eat fermented shark in their everyday lives, but nonetheless I do not want to accidentally chance upon this hákarl, minced up in some salad or chopped up and mixed with other foods and wrapped in a tortilla. I'm not your "crazy food" gal. When originally a friend was going to accompany me on this trip, she'd told me I'd have to eat "one gross thing." Now that she's not along with me, there is no such rule.

And really, all I want is a quick lunch. My seven-hour trip is already stretching beyond its planned boundaries, timewise; I want to get back on the road quickly. I find a bin with ready-made sandwiches and wraps, and what's more, many of them are labeled in both Icelandic and English. A chicken marsala wrap catches my eye but I continue to search through the options. As I do so, a woman pushes her way in front of me and yells in English to a friend, "Here, there are sandwiches here." She seems not to notice me at all. I grab the chicken marsala and make my way to the checkout.

Back in the parking lot, I eat my wrap in my car. I am parked just on the other side of the tour bus, facing it, and I see people re-embarking. After not too long, the woman from the sandwich bin appears and climbs into the bus. I am not surprised.

Here's one of the things about tour buses. If you think about these buses, carrying forty or fifty people, dumping them off for a limited amount of time at a site, calling them back at a specified time, with limited good seats and lots of crowding, I think they just lend themselves to cultivating this sort of pushiness. You have to push to get a good seat. You have to push to get to the sites. You have to push to get a good position for good pictures at the sites. And so on. Now, I know tour groups are right for some people.

Many people, in fact. Lots of people don't feel comfortable driving themselves around a foreign country. Many don't want to bother with a rental car. Others simply don't want to have to plan. All these things are valid. But if you take a tour bus, please remember to just take a breath occasionally and be patient. Your time and space are limited on the bus, but your compassion and humanity and graciousness need not be.

At Egilsstaðir, I try to gas up using a pre-paid gas card I'd bought earlier, but the pump won't take the pre-paid card and there's a long line inside the store. After just a few days of relative isolation, the gas station combined with the chaos of the Bónus have me a little claustrophobic. I don't really need gas yet, I decide. Surely there will be another station between here and Akureyri. I leave without gassing up.

On my way out, I drive across the bridge over Lake Lagarfljót and stop on the other side to look for any signs of monster life. It's truly unlikely here, as it's the tip of the lake and quite busy; if The Worm is going to make an appearance, I'm guessing it would more likely be somewhere else along the sixteen-mile-long lake. Still, I squint my eyes and look at the softly rippling surface of the water, watching for a giant worm. Somewhere, I'd read someone describe the water as "impossibly green." I had been imagining emerald green, dark green, but in fact this water is more of a milky green, in the way the waters of Blue Lagoon are an opaque milky blue. Barely green, at that, but it's possible it's the grayness of the day is dimming the brilliant green the other visitor saw. The sky has been overcast all day, with rain breaking through every now and then. In sunlight, maybe that's when a person would see the impossible green.

Either way, I do not see a worm. The world is safe from natural disasters for another day.

The drive to Egilsstaðir more or less makes up the first part of the day. In the second part, from Egilsstaðir to Akureyri, the road diverts a bit from the coastline. Here in the north-east, Highway 1 cuts across the country, leaving the far north-east to be served by lesser roads such as the 85, the 917. I am curious about that section of the country but had to limit myself; already I realize I have bitten off more of the country than a person can rightly chew in two weeks. To explore the full length and breadth of the country would require much more time.

Here, edging toward the center of Iceland, the landscape is still barren but in a different way. It's hillier than the coastline, but the roads are still narrow and there are still very few trees. The hilliness presents a challenge in passing other cars. At one point, I'm behind a camper van traveling along at a good 10 or 15 kph slower than I'd like to be going, but with the hills it's hard to see around the van to judge whether it's safe to pass. What's more, the van itself is the full width of the road, and the driver is clearly nervous about that. He frequently pushes into the oncoming lane, leaving less than a full lane-width of road on the other side, and making passing an even more precarious proposition. But, finally I make my way around, and speed off.

And then, off to the right, there's a pull-out. Several cars. What might this be? Why, it's an unexpected waterfall! I pull in with the other drivers who have discovered this spot, and end up taking off on a five-minute hike along narrow but well-traversed foot trails to see what I think is called Ysti-Rjúkandi. (It's a waterfall, but without "foss" in the name, so I'm not sure.) A steady stream of people is parking and pulling out of the tiny pull-out, surprised and delighted as I am that for once, there's an opportunity to get a closer look at something on the side of the road.

As I drive away, something occurs to me. It's quite fortuitous, actually, that I chose to drive the Ring Road counterclockwise. I could just as well have driven it clockwise. But as a solo driver driving counterclockwise, I've managed to keep most of the scenery on my left. All along the southern coast, with its coastline shelf and never-ending waterfalls, everything was to my left. Had I driven clockwise, it's quite possible I wouldn't have seen nearly as much; the shelf would have been hidden behind the roof of the car and I'd never have known many of the sights even existed. Down when I saw Rútshellir, the old dwelling off the side of the road, I don't know if it was easily visible from the other direction. If no cars had been present I might not have stopped. Therefore, my suggestion for drivers, especially those driving solo, who will not have a chance to trade off with a driving partner: Consider driving the Ring Road counterclockwise. I'm very glad I did.

Speaking of waterfalls, it's almost surprising I stopped for this one. Not entirely surprising, but just a bit. I suppose partially I stopped for a break in the driving — this day is getting very, very long. But also, I've always loved waterfalls. What's not to love? The crashing water, the misty spray, the infinitely various ways the water cascades over the rocks, each one beautiful. Here in Iceland, I'd say it would be nearly impossible to come and not see waterfalls. You'd have to try, really, or just go to a city (one without waterfalls) and stay there. There are waterfalls everywhere. Initially, I stopped to take pictures every time I could. But they've become so common on my trip that while I still mentally appreciate the falls, I simply admire them and drive on.

The day is getting long. What was supposed to be seven hours of driving has, of course, extended itself. I've been on the road seven hours now (short stops included), and I estimate I'm still a couple hours away from Akureyri. Is the landscape less interesting on the eastern side of the country, or am I immune to it, having seen it through endless miles already? Or is it the day, dark and cloud-covered, preventing me from seeing the beauty around me? I rethink my plan to drive the east coast, try to decide what I would do differently if I did it again, but my brain is tired. Long as the drive is, the roads don't get any wider. My attention is demanded.

I start to think about tour groups some more. If I were on a tour bus, of course, I could take a nap here. I could let someone else worry about passing slow camper vans, let someone else brave the roads in the rain. If, that is, any tour buses even come out this way. I think a bus tour along the eastern part of the Ring Road might be a bit of a harder sell than those in the south. Maybe it's the rain, which in turn hides the beauty of the country from me; maybe it's the countryside itself, but the word "mind-numbing" keeps popping into my consciousness.

For hikers, I should note that some of this area looks like it would make for gorgeous hiking. Jökuldalur ("the glacial valley") in particular seems worth a look, with its river Jökulsá á Brú. The area known as Kringilsárrani apparently is home to lots of reindeer. And so on. I think there's a lot to do and see in the east, but it might not be easily accessible for someone just passing through, like I am today.

At any rate, after much thinking and mind-meandering, I finally reach the approach to the Lake Mývatn area. ("Mývatn" = "midges," little flying bugs that can drive you crazy. I can never pronounce Mývatn quite right, but when I hear it, it sounds something like "Mee-vaht.")

There are many places I'd researched before the trip, and now that I'm finally here I'm always amazed that so many of those places are right along the road. This is the case with Námafjall, a steaming geothermal area that is on the left as I drive past. (It's getting late in the day and I'm anxious to be at my destination so I don't stop; besides, I'll be traveling this road again in two days.) It's actually signposted as Hverir, and to be honest I can't figure out if Námafjall and Hverir are the same thing, or one is the subset of another. Or maybe Hverir means "this way," for all I know. "Turn left here." Regardless, it's a landscape of rich dusty reds and browns, mottled with steaming chalky blue boiling mudpools. I will definitely stop when I'm here again on Sunday.

A large hill stands between Námafjall (or maybe the hill IS Námafjall?) and Lake Mývatn. As I reach the summit, I look down and see another Blue Lagoon-esque pool. On the right, it turns out, is a pool of very hot hot springs, the waters edged by foamy white sulfuric minerals. These pools, I believe, are part of a geothermal power plant. The actual Mývatn Nature Baths, the ones you can soak in, are off to the left instead. Another stop for Sunday.

And then, at long last, I reach Lake Mývatn and its immediate surrounds. I am instantly charmed. One side of my family gets together every three years, and I think to myself that if we all lived in Iceland, I'd insist that we meet up here one year. It has the feel of a summer resort area, a quieter one that perhaps gets colder than many resort areas, but beautiful and with room to hike and walk and do lakeside yoga for days. Not that I do lakeside yoga, but here, you totally could. The land formations in this area have become more interesting again, huge ragged chunks of lava with enticing cracks leading to crevices and caves just asking to be explored, decorating the scenery along my route. I drive through, growing weary but feeling slightly re-energized knowing I'm nearly done for the day.

And finally, I'm on the last approach to Akureyri. My GPS has a feature that tells me the estimated time of arrival, and every day I watch the estimated time get later and later as I drive. Stops have increased my total time, but also, I'm obviously not driving as fast as my GPS thinks I should. I lose minutes continuously along the way, but eventually, I am just minutes away.

I am fatigued, it is Friday afternoon, traffic heading into Akureyri is thick. And I am driving along the edge of a cliff, a drop-off to my right, cars piling up behind me. For once, there is no room for them to pass safely, but I can't bring myself to go any faster than I am. I am tense, stressed, wishing I could pull over and let everyone by. I am tired. All I want is to reach the apartment.

And finally, after curving around and across the long sweep of the bottom of the fjord on which Akureyri sits, I do. With a great sigh of relief I turn the car up a lonely back road to the complex, and turn in.

Okay, people. This is what I want to know: Is it just me, or does everyone show up at hotels looking like they've been through the ringer backwards? On my first day here, I'd spent seven uncomfortable and tiring hours on a plane, then went to Blue Lagoon, which is already notorious for wreaking havoc on one's hair, especially long hair, but on top of that the masseuse put oil in my hair to do a scalp massage. Then I spent the day wandering around, including twenty minutes at Gullfoss, with whipping winds and mist. By the time I got to Mary Frances's house, I looked like hákarl warmed over. You may think, well, that was the first day and with the flight, that's normal. Right? But I swear to you, every day here I start the day looking reasonably put together, but by the time I get to my hotels I look like no one ever taught me how to comb my hair or dress myself. What happens?

But, it doesn't matter. The front desk clerk is pleasant and friendly. I am here.

I'm staying at the Sæluhús Apartments. In my tired state, on walking into the apartment I see more flaws than I might otherwise. The studio apartment has a small kitchen, with oven, microwave, dishwasher, pots and pans, and a full set of dishes (including the very important wine glasses, which I vow to use). However, a couple glasses look like they were put away dirty. I'd wanted to wash clothes tonight for my meeting with Akureyri's mayor tomorrow morning, but the front desk clerk has told me there's only one washer and one dryer for the dozens of studio apartments. And the blackout curtains are actually blinds; they do the job well enough, but I can tell some light will seep around the edges. To top it off, the last visitor's garbage wasn't taken out of the bathroom.

But, I am resilient, these things are small and just part of traveling, and I can manage. I wash the unwashed dishes, and set my alarm for first thing in the morning so I can catch the washer and dryer empty (I hope). The apartment is generally nice, in a good area (though I might like to be closer to downtown), and I'm overjoyed at not having to repack for three days.

Nine hours of driving, and it's times like this I ask myself: "Why?" and "Was it worth it?" "Would I do it again?"

So let's start with Why.

Why. Why indeed did I drive for nine hours across the east of Iceland? Through landscape both fascinating and monotonous — at the same time? Driving in areas so remote that in the first half of the trip I passed about one car coming the other way per minute, on average, and later in the trip, about one car every minute and a half? Driving past spots I'll be driving to again in two days?

Well, my friend, you ask a lot of questions. Let's slow down.

I'm here in Akureyri for three nights. Three glorious nights. This means I don't have to unpack tonight and repack tomorrow. This means I can settle in a bit and get to know the area. This means that, despite the fact that the washer is occupied right now, I can do laundry at some point in the next few days. And believe me, these clothes need some washing! Sure, I can wash things out in the sink, but try air-drying jeans once (after washing them in the sink, without a spin cycle) and you'll know why that's not a great option. Being here for three nights means that for about seventy-two hours, I have a place I can call home. I do sometimes choose to spend only one night in a town, but it's not my preference. It's too transitory. So if the nine-hour drive means I can stay one more night in the same place, that's good. The idea of a restful vacation sounds wonderful, going one place and staying there for two weeks. But I know I'll never be able to do it. If I'm all the way here, in Iceland, who knows when I'll be back? How can I justify missing something when I'm only an hour away? And so I push, and I get tired. While I'm doing it I love it, but at the end of the day I'm exhausted. Occasional rest days are critical.

However. Nine hours is a heck of a lot of driving, especially for me. I don't generally relish long drives; I really only do it when I'm traveling, to get from one place to the next. After today's drive, I am exhausted and going cross-eyed. And, I'll admit it, due to my fatigue at the end of the day, my driving was probably not at its best. Driving such a long day probably wasn't the smartest plan, and no, I don't think I'll plan a seven-which-becomes-nine-hour driving day ever again, not without sharing the driving with a companion.

As far as the east of Iceland, specifically, would I drive it again? You know, any place you go has its beauty and its treasures. From what I could see, you may have to look a little more closely in the east to find the gems. I don't want to say they're not here, because I'm sure they are. I think it might just take a little more time to discover them. The fjord I passed just before turning off onto the 939 gravel road, where the swans were, had a cute little village that looked like it could be fun to visit, and I'm sure there are plenty more towns just like that. Rather than driving the whole way from south to north, though, I might be inclined to take a domestic flight in from Reykjavík to Egilsstaðir, and explore the north-east and south-east from there. This drive was very long.

Just for the record, it should be noted there are no gas stations between Egilsstaðir and Mývatn. Fill up when you can. I got from Höfn to Akureyri with about a quarter to a third of a tank left.

Once I'm settled, I make a quick trip to a Bónus for groceries. Then, back at my apartment, I get online. I want to look at the route I drove to see about that damn gravel road from Hades. It is, as I noted earlier, a shortcut to avoid driving the long way around on Highway 1. The Ring Road, Highway 1, follows the coastline in that part of the country, whereas 939 cuts up and over the mountain. A much shorter route.

But here's the thing, people, and I think these are important things:

1. If I'd stayed on Highway 1, the gravel road would have ended soon and I'd have been back on paved road in just a few miles. From what I can, tell it does revert back to gravel road after a while, but I'm assuming it's not the white-knuckle hairpin-turn high-grade gravel road of 939.

2. The travel distance to drive Highway 1 vs. Highway 939 is about 60 kilometers longer. BUT:

3. The travel TIME for Highway 1 vs. Highway 939 is about 8 minutes longer. EIGHT MINUTES. Considering the route took about a year off my life, I think I could have spared those eight minutes. And I wouldn't have been on the verge of throwing up/peeing my pants/crying the whole time, either, I suspect. And what's more, the reports are that the coastal route (Ring Road route) is more scenic, too.

Thanks, GPS. You owe me.

Of all the things I've planned for this trip, I was most anxious about today's drive. I'd envisioned routes along the cliff's edge, gravel roads, hours of white-knuckle driving.

I was right. Still, it wasn't as bad as I'd anticipated. And now, it's over. For three days, Akureyri is home.

Sites I had on my list for today, but didn't get to or see:

Búlandstindur: This is a pyramid-shaped mountain in the east, which supposedly has mystic power. I was not planning to go to it; I just had it on my list to watch for as I drove by. Due to the overcast day, I didn't see a thing. Nor did I witness any mystic power. Unfortunately.

Skjoldolfsstadhahnukur: I wrote this down more as a reminder to watch for reindeer than anything else. I think it's a reindeer farm?

Dimmuborgir: Two main reasons I didn't go there: (1) by the time I got in the general area, I was exhausted and ready to just get to Akureyri; and (2) due to my lack of research beforehand, I didn't really know where it was. Dimmuborgir means "dark castles" and is apparently an area where the lava formations are particularly beautiful and castle-like. From what I can tell, when you hit Lake Mývatn at Reykjahlíð and the Ring Road goes around the lake to the right (to the north), you instead take 848 south. After about three miles there's a road named "Dimmuborgir" so I'm guessing that's where you turn. It looks beautiful. Go there and report back.

Also in the Lake Lagarfljót area: Hallormsstaðarskógur, the biggest forest in Iceland; Hengifoss, one of the tallest waterfalls in Iceland; and the nearby waterfall Litlanesfoss, set deep within an array of hexagonal basalt columns.

Akureyri

Saturday, August 3, 2013

5 a.m., and I am awake, without help of my alarm. I have not seen true darkness since I got here. Does it ever get fully dark at this time of year? If it does, it must be very late or very early. I've been too tired to stay up past 10 p.m. to try to find out.

I'm starting to judge hotels based on their blackout curtains as much as anything else.

I think I slightly miss nighttime. The cozy, comforting cloak of darkness is a trigger that tells my brain it's time to sleep. Throughout each night here, I wake up multiple times. This is normal at home, too, but here, the dim light throughout the night confuses my sense of time. Every time I wake up, I have to check the clock to see whether it's actually morning, or if I have hours yet to sleep. The light streaming behind the curtains at 3 a.m. could just as well be the light at 6 a.m. Still, it's fun and unique and interesting to have light all night, and I imagine if I lived here (and therefore weren't exhausted at night from such busy days) I might indulge in some crazy midnight sun activities outside, just because I could.

Since I'm awake, I get up to do laundry. As expected, no one else was trying to do laundry at 5 a.m., so my wash is done early, much to my relief. The only scheduled appointment on my agenda is interviewing Akureyri's mayor, Eiríkur Björn Björgvinsson, at 11 a.m. After that, I'll explore Akureyri, write, and relax.

The thought of a day without travel feels luxurious, decadent. There's a mist on the morning and it'll probably drizzle all day. Tomorrow is my day to travel around the region, do the "Diamond Circle," and it looks like it might rain again. I'm not too eager to drive some of those roads when they're wet, but we'll see how it goes. Today, I'll rest.

And I think my brain needs it. When I got up today, I saw that I'd put a coffee filter over the antenna box on the TV. I know the way my brain works; I know what happened. In the middle of the night, I'm sure I was convinced that the hotel was spying on me through the antenna box. I got up, got a coffee filter that I'd seen in the cupboard earlier (though at the time I'd thought they were napkins), and draped one over the box.

It happens.

But I think a day off will do me some good.

9 a.m. Laundry is done. Now: shower. Good glory be, this shower! I have never experienced so much magnificent water pressure. It is divine. Any of you with thick, long hair will understand the frustration of showers that trickle, the way you never quite get your hair or scalp clean. Not so with this shower! I think it took off a layer of my skin with it, and after five days of travel, I'm delighted about that. It takes me a while to realize I can, and probably should, reduce the pressure a bit; when I got out, due to the construction of the shower (no lip to hold the water in), the water is

all over the bathroom floor. My room didn't come with a bathmat (oversight? or normal?), so I use a hand towel to try to mop up the flood. But the water pressure was totally worth it. I will remember this shower for a very long time. When I turn the water off at the end of my shower, I slightly overshoot and discover that turning the knob the other way turns on the overhead rain shower showerhead. !!! So that may be on the agenda tomorrow. A rain shower showerhead (surely it's actually called something else?) is on the list of things my future dream house will have.

10 a.m. Time to head out to meet the mayor. Yes, I am very early. Our meeting is at 11, but I'm ready now and I'm just twiddling my thumbs, eager to get started on the interview. In theory, the meeting place is only five or ten minutes away, but I want to allow plenty of time to get lost, find my way, figure out parking. First I'll find where I need to go; then I'll wander around Akureyri to fill up whatever time I need to fill before returning to City Hall for the interview.

My GPS, always defiant, is persnickety about helping me get there. If I type in Geislagata 9 (the address Eiríkur gave me), it tells me it can find Geislagata 8 and Geislagata 10 but not Geislagata 9. When I zoom out from the map view, though, there's a Geislagata 9 available. Oh, GPS. You are not amusing me. I drive to what supposedly is Geislagata 9, and park in the disturbingly empty parking lot. It's Saturday, after all, but Eiríkur chose this day, so mustn't it be an okay day for our interview? Do I have the wrong place?

The front of the building says "Ráðhús." I vaguely recall that the German word "Rathaus" means "City Hall" in English. Plus, there's a signboard outside which says "City Hall" at the top. I may not always be the sharpest knife in the drawer, but from these clues I'm fairly certain I'm where I'm supposed to be. Deciding that maybe I'm just early, I take a brief drive around the area to see what can be seen.

I drive out from City Hall and back, returning after every few roads so I don't lose track of where I want to be. (Yes, I know, it's a small town and I shouldn't be able to get lost, but I don't want to miss my appointment.) At one point I end up down at the waterfront, at the visitor centre. The rain-soaked parking lot is empty here, too, but I take my chances. Maybe I'm the only visitor in town today? But no. I walk up to the door and discover a sign taped to it: The visitor centre is closed today. Closed on a summer Saturday? Is that normal? It seems a bit unwelcoming, I suppose. On the other hand, much of the town seems to be shut down. I don't see many people out either walking or driving. Maybe it's the rain? Is everyone inside somewhere at a party I don't know about? Why is the town so dead today?

I walk along the waterfront a bit — it looks like it must be beautiful in the sunshine — and then decide to return to the Ráðhús. It's just a little before 11 a.m. by now. There's a doorway with a bit of an alcove for protection from the weather, but I want to be visible in case someone comes by looking for me (or for anyone). I stand in the rain (I even get out my umbrella, it's that rainy) at the front door. I walk around the building. A police car comes by a couple times and seems to pause briefly to look at me, but apparently I don't look quite suspicious enough for them to stop. I ponder what I could do to look more suspicious, so they might come help me. I try all the doors of the building; none is unlocked. I ring what might be a doorbell, but without much hope. Nothing happens. The building is clearly closed.

How long is a person supposed to wait for a mayor in the rain? I decide twenty minutes is enough (in college, we gave professors fifteen minutes, so an extra five seems fair), and then I do what any self-respecting woman who has been stood up by a mayor would do: I make my way to the wine and liquor store.

When I was at Bónus yesterday, I asked a man who was stocking shelves where a person might go to get liquor. (My search of all the aisles at Bónus came up with nothing.) "There's only one place," he'd said. "Vínbúðin." Actually, when he said it I totally didn't understand what he said, but I looked it up and now I know it was Vínbúðin. It is, in fact, the only place, countrywide, where you can buy beer, wine, or any form of alcohol. Outside the greater Reykjavík area, there are only about three dozen Vínbúðin stores, or Vínbúðir, as seems to be the plural, so plan accordingly.

(Crazy fact: beer was banned in Iceland from 1915 to 1989. 1989! That's practically yesterday! Wine and spirits were only banned from 1915 to 1935, but beer made it all the way to 1989. This is fine for me, as I think beer is gross, but that is a very long time for a very cold country to go without beer.)

The Vínbúðin store opened at 11. I drove by it on my way down to City Hall, but obviously was no one there yet. Now it's buzzing with people looking to imbibe this weekend, and I'm one of them.

I wander the aisles a bit, look to see if I could find any Washington wines (I won't buy a Washington wine; I'm just curious whether they have any). I have my eye on a Riesling for today, but I don't know the brands available here. I surreptitiously watch people buying Rieslings (there are a lot of people buying alcohol!), to see which they prefer. Finally, I decide just to ask someone who works there, so I find a clerk. The one I talk to first knows beer, not wine. And, she looks just like Björk. I'm not entirely certain what Björk looks like, actually; I probably wouldn't recognize her outside her swan outfit. But this woman looks like what I think Björk looks like. This is not to say that Björk knows nothing about wine. Just that the woman who looks like Björk only knows beer.

Another woman, who does not look like Björk, helps me, and she deftly points out that some of the wines have cork tops, and some have screw tops. Ah! Very important. I hadn't checked the kitchen cabinets for a corkscrew, and I don't want to make any assumptions. One time, a long time ago, right out of college, a friend and I bought some wine before realizing we didn't have a corkscrew. We then went to my landlady to see if she had one, at which point she reminded me, "We're Mormon." (Who apparently don't drink. Which I learned that day.) We then ended up trying a screw and a screwdriver to get the cork out. FYI, I do not recommend this. What do I recommend instead? Buying wine with a screw top.

Having picked a Riesling with a screw top, I browse the store a bit. I quickly notice a man with a grocery cart full of wine. FULL. I smile and give him a knowing nod.

He says something in Icelandic.

I say, "Party?"

He says, "Fishing trip."

I look at the cart. "Looks like a very good fishing trip!"

He laughs. "For sixteen people. For four days."

I count at least fifty bottles. "Fishing" trip indeed! They must plan to get the fish drunk to make them easier to catch! How do I get myself invited on that one? I roughly calculate the expense in my head. That is one expensive fishing trip.

At the counter, I finally give in to the currency. I have been using bills more than coins, simply because it's easier to pull out a bill than to count out the unfamiliar coins. But I've accumulated quite a heavy handful of coins and I try to pay with them instead. Sensing I am taking too long, I finally just put my hand out to the clerk. "Can you help me find the right coins?" I ask in amused desperation. He laughs and picks out what he needs. (I pay enough attention to know he chose the right coins, but I would not have expected otherwise. A very honest people, these Icelanders.)

I go on my merry way, bottle in hand, ready at last for my day of rest. I head up the hill to a different grocery store just to check it out, as I've only been to Bónus stores and little gas station stores so far. I consider the chocolate-covered banana snacks, but end up only getting the milk I forgot last night.

I've developed a way to let people know I can't speak Icelandic, without having to say, "I don't speak Icelandic. Do you speak English?" Because that would get old really fast. So instead, when I know I'm about to interact with someone (in this case the store clerk), I'll give 'em a big old smile and speak first. Anything will do. "How are you today?" works fine. Immediately they get it, and to talk to me in English, and they do all speak English, thank goodness. Smiles are universal.

I approach the grocery store counter and greet the clerk with, "Hello, how are you?" The clerk, true to form, smiles and speaks English to me. "I am good." I pay with my credit card. I'm using my credit card far more than I like to when I travel, but I'm not encountering a lot of ATMs so I don't have much cash. Luckily, I've not encountered "dynamic currency conversion" (DCC) at all. DCC is this thing where in a foreign (to you) country, they'll offer to charge your credit card in your home currency, for your "convenience," so you will know how much you're paying. It's tempting, because it's hard to do the currency conversion yourself, on the fly, in your head, while you're trying to quickly finish a transaction. The thing they often don't tell you is that when you agree to this they can add on an extra fee for this "convenience." How much it is depends on your bank and the company, but basically you're paying more if you pay in your own currency (in my case, U.S. dollars or USD) than if you paid in the local currency. I've run into DCC in other countries, but not once in Iceland. Every charge has been in Icelandic krona, ISK, and no one has even given me the option to pay in USD. It's a relief not to have to worry about fighting over the charge, because whenever I do it's always uncomfortable. Sometimes the cashiers don't even know you have a choice, or they'll argue with you about whether they can void the original charge, and it's just awkward. I do know, however, that my credit card company will automatically charge me a fee for every foreign transaction — so many different possible fees! — so I feel a bit guilty over all the credit card use. But, it's convenient. Note to self: Try to remember to find an ATM and get some more cash.

Driving back to my apartment, I finally see what I've been watching for: a heart-shaped red light in a stoplight. I've heard about these but hadn't seen any yet. Apparently, when the economy crashed in 2008, the people of Akureyri got together to figure out what they could do to help improve everyone's morale, to try to get through the rough times. One thing they did was start putting up hearts everywhere — decals in store windows and such. The city got on board and converted the plain old circular red stoplights into heart-shaped red stoplights. I had not yet seen any down in the center of town; it's possible I missed them due to being more concerned about not getting lost, but I don't recall seeing any. It is surprisingly uplifting to see one. Way to go, Akureyri!

When I get back to the apartment, I see the mayor has been trying to get in touch with me via email, starting about fifteen minutes after I left. He's had a family emergency and had to fly out of town, and hopes to reschedule. I write back with my schedule for the coming days, saying that if we can't find time, I understand. I'm disappointed, but glad to know he didn't just forget about me.

So now I get down to the serious business of relaxing. I'd planned to spend the day "downtown," but having found it surprisingly empty, and with not just the town but also the mood dampened by the rain, I decide a day in is just what the doctor ordered. On the clock it's just noon, but it's five o'clock somewhere, so I make myself a sandwich and open the screw-top Riesling.

I begin watching online videos about Iceland, to see what I can learn about where I've been and where I'm going. Amidst the videos of polar bear attacks and volcanic eruptions and the Eurovision singing contest (huge in Europe) are some really interesting segments. Iceland is, I learn, the last country in Europe to have been discovered and settled by man. We all know about the Vikings, but actually Iceland was first settled by Irish monks, looking for some peace and quiet. The Vikings were the ones who stuck it out in the harsh environment, though; their first settlements on the land were around the ninth century. What this means, interestingly, or at least interestingly to me, is that Iceland is really a rather young country (both geologically and in human settlement terms). I remember years ago, when I was in England, we drove past a school in York, and I swear I remember reading it was established in the fifth or sixth century. I remember this, because I remember wondering what the curriculum in 400 or 500 could possibly have been. I mean, that is old. Or older yet, Newgrange in Ireland, which was built somewhere around 3200 B.C.E. Civilization in Iceland is practically new in comparison. Further evidence of the country's youth comes in the form of its old buildings: There aren't many. Only rarely will you see ruins, and they're not that old. The overgrown turf houses are generally the oldest buildings; some say the turf houses at Keldur, which my GPS refused to take me to, are the oldest houses in Iceland, having been built at the tail end of the twelfth century. Obviously, the Vikings lived in structures of some sort before that, but those structures are no longer around. On occasion while driving on this trip, I've surmised that Iceland is in some ways like a combination of Switzerland and Ireland (we judge by what we know, after all, and those are two countries I've been to). One main difference, though, is that in driving around Europe you are constantly coming upon old stone buildings, in various degrees of disrepair. Here, however, you simply have land, land, and more land. I've wondered why the ancient people didn't build with lava, but probably there's some structural reason for it (the uneven sides and porous nature of lava among those reasons). Or perhaps they did, and then a volcano blew up and covered all their handiwork.

At any rate, there are few truly old buildings or ruins.

Currently, Iceland's population rests at just about 320,000, with more than a third of that living in Reykjavík proper and a total of nearly 200,000 in the greater Reykjavík area. Iceland is small in size, just under 40,000 square miles, a little smaller than Kentucky and a little bigger than Indiana. This could change, though, as the country is still being formed. It is home to more than one hundred and thirty volcanic mountains, causing frequent eruptions and earthquakes. These volcanoes also provide plentiful geothermal power, giving a fantastic source of both power and heat for Icelanders. More than ninety percent of homes in Iceland utilize geothermal power for heat.

I'm surprised to learn that Iceland has a tremendous problem with soil erosion. Iceland is even home to Europe's biggest desert. You heard me. Europe's biggest desert is in Iceland. Nearly a third of the country is officially classified as desert. I've been fascinated since the moment I landed by the complete lack of trees on this island, but apparently it wasn't always that way. It's estimated that when people first settled this land, anywhere from thirty to sixty percent of the land (probably closer to thirty) was covered in woodland, mostly lush birch forests. Now, it's less than one percent.

It would be simple to say that the first Viking settlers deforested the land, but the reality is more complex than that. Unmanaged sheep grazing, climate changes, natural disturbances, and human use, among other factors, all contributed to the problem, in some places causing a total loss of vegetation and the underlying soil. What I had been thinking was land on which dirt had not yet been built up, might in fact be land from which all the soil has blown away. Regardless of the causes, though, the question is, what must Icelanders do to reverse the damage? Iceland sits as a cautionary tale now for other countries. Studies have shown that soil samples from Iceland blow as easily in the wind as soil samples from the moon. Tree planting efforts have begun; the first tree was planted in Reykjavík in 1884, and while work toward this effort remains, the city has a good number of trees. Other restoration efforts are in place around the country, including well-intentioned widespread plantings of lupine starting around 1945. Unfortunately, as is often the case with introduced species, the lupine spreads so quickly it is now considered invasive, preventing other vegetation from taking hold; efforts are underway in some places to remove it. Iceland faces a challenge in the coming years, but it seems that Icelanders, who place a high value on conservation and the environment, are tackling the problem with typical Icelandic resourcefulness and determination.

On another note, but still speaking of Icelandic resourcefulness and determination, let's talk about bananas.

You know how you notice things, but don't really notice that you're noticing things, until suddenly you're like, "Hey! I've been noticing this thing for a while now!" That's how it is with me and bananas in Iceland.

I'd say I noticed the banana candy first. At the check-out counters, they often have these chocolate-coated banana candies, common enough that you know it must be popular. And then I just started to notice bananas everywhere, enough that I thought, Icelanders really are obsessed with bananas! I thought it must be the novelty of bananas or something — after all, bananas are a tropically grown fruit, right? So it must be a thing where Icelanders crave the tropics and thus … import bananas and make banana candy. Or something. Right? Last night, when I was shopping, I was struck by all the banana products, but then today, on my way back from being stood up by the mayor, I finally realized I had been noticing the prevalence of bananas for days. So now, I'm doing some research.

And guess what? Iceland, in fact, grows bananas.

Well, people in Iceland grow bananas. The country itself lacks thumbs.

Anyway. Coming from the great Pacific Northwest, where we have some of the world's best farmers markets, with luscious produce available locally and seasonally, I might say that the produce in Iceland generally leaves something to be desired. (No offense intended, Iceland; we all have our strengths.) However, I learned today that due to its fabulous geothermal energy and heat, Iceland actually can grow some greenhouse/hothouse produce with much success. Some articles claim that Iceland is Europe's top banana producer, but further research tells me that's not the case; Spain is. Some articles claim Iceland exports bananas, while others say that's false. There are stories, even, that an overabundance of bananas has on occasion caused the price of bananas to drop so low that some farmers have burned bananas just to create scarcity. I couldn't find proof of that, but it's an interesting tale. It's hard to determine the exact status of Iceland's banana growing and import/export status, but the fact remains: Iceland both loves and grows bananas. Who knew!

I did not, however, buy any bananas on my shopping trip yesterday. What I did buy was something labeled pottbrauð. I could tell it was a bread, though I did not know what kind. I guessed that "pott" might imply it was baked in a pot (rather than being made with marijuana, which seemed unlikely), but that didn't tell me anything about what kind of bread it might be. It just looked like a rich, dense, dark bread, so I bought it. (I figured I could be fairly certain there is no fermented shark in this.) Turns out the bread is quite delicious, and on researching it, I find it is indeed bread traditionally made in a pot; in this case, it is rúgbrauð, or rye bread. People used to — and occasionally still do — make the bread by steaming it at a thermal hot spring for up to twenty-four hours, thus caramelizing some of the sugars within. I can taste that mild sweetness in this loaf; it is delicious. However, I also read that another nickname for rúgbrauð is þrumari — which roughly translates to "thunder bread." This is not because the thunder god Thor used to make this bread on his days off, but rather because excessive consumption of the bread causes, well, let's just call it natural thunder. I vow to take it easy on the thunder bread so as not to disturb the neighbors.

The weather today remains wet. I have a bit of a view out my balcony, but it's a view of the rain. Up here in the north, it's colder too. Mary Frances tells me Reykjavík has two seasons: winter and waiting for summer. There are, she says, about ten nice days in summer. If that's the case in Akureyri, as well, then this, I think to myself, isn't one of them. I pride myself on the fact that coming from Seattle, I can travel in any weather. I'm used to gray, overcast days, after all. Maybe it's the thought of having to deal with wet clothes that stops me from venturing out, but whatever it is, I stay in.

After not too long, the bottle of wine is down to half full. I've taken a nap, chatted with friends online once they woke up back home, and am generally feeling refreshed. I spend the evening organizing my luggage, reading, writing, and researching the rest of my trip. Tomorrow, on to the Diamond Circle.

Notes:

Akureyri is, I'm told, the one area outside of Reykjavík where parking is regulated. Parking is still free, but you have to put a parking disk on display in your car. It's basically a clock, and you set it to the time you arrived so they know when to ticket you. Disks are available free from banks, hotels, guesthouses, and shops, so just be sure you get one when you get to town, and then use it when you park in the central core.

Akureyri has a good number of museums for all interests, and of course it has its own iconic church, too, Akureyrarkirkja, or "Akureyri church." If you need more turf houses in your life, you can also head about thirty kilometers north of Akureyri (on the other side of the fjord), to Grenivík, to see the Laufás Turf Homes.

The Diamond Circle

Sunday, August 4, 2013

The sun seems confused today, trying to decide whether to show up or not. I am hopeful it will come out, but either way, I'm back out into the wonders of Iceland!

Driving out of Akureyri today on the road I drove in on two days ago, the difference is night and day, black and white, fatigued and refreshed. When I arrived, I was at the ragged tail end of nine long hours of driving, and my eyes and brain and focus were exhausted. Two days ago, I was driving south on the Ring Road on the east side of Eyjafjörður — the longest fjord in Iceland, with Akureyri sitting on its southwest coast. The road is steep, and I was on the outside edge, and I was so weary that I was gripping the steering wheel and driving as slowly as I could, anxious about Friday afternoon traffic piling up behind me but unwilling to push beyond what my travel-tired mind could handle. It felt precarious and frightening, and yesterday the memories of the drive and the thought of having to go on that road again had me seriously considering joining a tour bus to do today's route, just so I wouldn't have to drive it again.

Today, though, I am refreshed and strong, and driving out is a breeze. Granted, this time I'm on the inside, the hill side, rather than the fall-over-the-cliff side, but still it's clear to me that taking a day off from driving was wise. I'm ready to travel again, and today will be a treat, I hear: Iceland's Diamond Circle, the scenic road route that contains all the gems of the north. Another full day ahead, but each stop is relatively close to the others, so I know the driving won't seem too tedious. I hope.

Back when I first arrived and Car Rental Guy was going over the Big Map with me, I mentioned the Diamond Circle. He'd never heard of it. He knew the sites themselves — the fishing town of Húsavík, the waterfalls Goðafoss and Dettifoss, and the horseshoe canyon Ásbyrgi being the four main points — but had never heard the term "Diamond Circle." So, Diamond Circle tourism board, there's work yet to be done!

Regardless of what Car Rental Guy knows, I have heard of the Diamond Circle and I'm about to embark on it. It's a loop of about one hundred and sixty miles, plus thirty miles or so each way from Akureyri, so it's a full day. I'm so glad to be here in summer when I know that no matter how early I start, or how late I drive, I'll have daylight. (I've seen warnings, by the way, about driving west in summer. Because the sunsets are so very long, you have the sun in your eyes for a very long time. When I drove in, however, it was overcast the whole time, so I didn't have to worry about that.) I'm out the door by shortly after 7 a.m. After driving around yesterday, I'm down to less than a quarter of a tank and I need to get gas, so I stop at the N1 station that's just at the entrance to Akureyri. I'd previously bought an N1 gas card — you can get them in denominations of 3000, 5000, or 10,000 ISK. 5000 ISK (about $41) will only buy me a little more than half a tank, I estimate, but 10,000 ISK might be too much for the tank, so I've been buying the 5000 ISK cards to ensure I don't end up with gas cards I can't use.

Well, here's the thing. I'm still figuring this out, but as far as I can tell, there are both N1 stations with stores attached, and N1 stations with standalone gas pumps, like the Orkan stations I tried on my second day out. From what I've seen, and today confirms it, if the N1 station has a store attached, then it won't accept the gas cards; you have to use your credit card with your chip-and-PIN, or go inside the store.

This station won't take the gas card, but the store doesn't open until 8 a.m. There's no way I'm going to wait forty-five minutes for the station to open up. Surely there will be another gas station along the way. I ask my GPS, and it tells me there are stations to the north (a diversion from my planned route), or thirty miles away at Goðafoss, my first stop of the day. I'm sure I can get thirty miles on the gas I have, but I'm still a little nervous. Get gas when you can in Iceland. Pam's number one advice: Get gas when you can.

I drove right by Goðafoss on my way into Akureyri two days ago. You can't miss it; even I couldn't miss it. When I get there today it's just barely 8, and I delight in the fact there are only two other cars in the lot, with another pulling in right behind me.

It is cold. I realize it is the north, and I realize there's the word "ice" in "Iceland," but so far I've been lulled by rather mild weather. The early morning chill has not yet lifted, though, and the wind is blowing, and it is downright cold. Still, Goðafoss is beautiful. The story of Goðafoss, "waterfall of the gods," is that around the year 1000, Þorgeir Ljósvetningagoði declared that Christianity would henceforth be the official religion of Iceland, and then he threw his statues of the Norse gods into this waterfall. Goðafoss has a rather short drop, relative to some waterfalls I've seen so far; Seljalandsfoss and Skógafoss are both about five times as high, and Gullfoss drops just short of three times as far. But at Goðafoss, however short the drop, the river Skjálfandafljót spills over a wide arch before continuing along its way, making for a spectacular display.

Did I mention, however, that it is cold? And windy. The spray from the waterfall stings my face. I get back in the car and crank up the heat.

Just across the bridge, on the other side of Goðafoss from its main parking lot, there's a restaurant, hostel, and a gas station, an N1. This N1 station does not have an attached store, so I am hopeful my gas card will work here. To my relief, it does. I'd had a full 5000 ISK card and a partially used 5000 ISK card. I pump both into my tank, ending up with about 7000 ISK before the cards run out. The gas gauge is nearly on full, so I am satisfied. This is plenty to get me around the Diamond Circle and back to Akureyri, where I will gas up again immediately on my return if the store is still open when I get there. Lesson learned.

The next stop is my second attempt at seeing turf houses, having missed out on finding Keldur. This time I'm headed to Grenjaðarstaður. (Note for when you are searching for these words online: You don't have to know where to find the ð or the Þ on your keyboard. If it's a ð, just type d. For ö, you can get away with o. For Þ, as in Þingvellir, type Th, or Thingvellir. And so on. For example, to find Grenjaðarstaður, you can just type Grenjadarstadur, and the search engine will know what you mean. I learned this early on, much to my relief!)

I travel north on Highway 845 to Grenjaðarstaður, where there are several attached (to each other) turf-roofed farmhouses, and a nineteenth-century church. The farmhouses and church sit in a wide valley, and were covered in turf to help insulate them from the icy wind. Today the weather is windy and somewhat miserable and very cold, and I commend the ingenuity of the people who built these types of houses. I can imagine that inside the farmhouses (which I don't think are in use today), it is cozy and warm, despite the chill and stinging rain.

A modern house sits very close to the turf-roofed farmhouses, so the farmhouses are now sort of sandwiched between the church and the house. The house seems to be occupied, generally, though I don't see any signs of life today. Is it a caretaker? A museum? I don't know.

I have no company at Grenjaðarstaður. It is indeed an isolated spot. I can imagine why storytelling became such an art form in this country. People gathered inside cozy homes, insulated from the harsh weather outside by their earth-covered houses. A little turf fire, a cup of tea, some rúgbrauð, and a long winter's night; what better to do than invent and share sagas of the times long gone?

Onward through the rain, continuing north on Highway 845 until it joins 85, to the northern coastal town of Húsavík, known as the whale watching capital of the world. I hadn't initially planned to stop in Húsavík; something about it just didn't interest me, and I'm not generally interested in whale watching tours. However, when I get here, I instantly fall in love with the tiny town, home to about 2,300 people. Húsavík is famous not just for whale watching in summer (and fishing throughout the year), but also for its lovely wooden church, Húsavíkurkirkja. (You may see a theme from the churches I've mentioned: the "kirkja" on the end of a word means it is a church.) A steady trickle of tourists is tromping up the stairs from the boating docks below the main road, launching grounds of all the whale watching tours. A row of ticket huts stands ready to sell me whatever tour I might wish to go on, but instead I head inside the church to see what can be seen, and to escape the chilly mist. Inside, sitting in pews and standing in aisles, almost every person is holding up a camera to get pictures of the interior. I climb the stairs tucked along the side of the entrance (stairs must be climbed!) to see where they lead, and find the balcony. Others, who either hadn't noticed the stairs or weren't sure if they were allowed to climb, follow behind me and soon the tiny balcony pews feel somewhat crowded. I notice there are more stairs, leading up to the bell tower, I'm sure, but they're roped off. This thwarts my inner "stairs must be climbed" urge, and I stare longingly up the stairway, then head back to the main level and out into the town.

Across the street, there's a little tourist shop, full of souvenirs and every possible thing you don't need. I am not generally a shopper, and hopefully by now the people who know me have learned not to expect me to bring home souvenirs for them. However, this shop is full of so many delights. Mittens, hand-knit in Húsavík, with fingertip pockets that fold back so you can use your fingers when you need them, then cover up again. Hats, the kind of Nordic-looking hats with the long hanging tails down either side, you know the ones, which surely my niece and nephew cannot live without. Lacy scarves and warm scarves. Books and DVDs spilling over with magnificent pictures of Iceland. Jackets and gloves and magnets and playing cards and all the things, and for some reason I am tempted. But then I remember myself, and I remember my bank account, and I put away the hats and mittens that had found their way into my hands. I do need another stamp to mail another letter, so I buy one from the clerk. And then it's time for tea.

I head down the wooden steps to the boat dock area. Down here, there are a couple cozy coffee houses, so I pick one and go inside. It's Sunday and some places seem to be closed, but this café is full to the brim; all the tables are occupied. I place my order and head outside to wait in the crisp air.

When the young woman comes out with my tea, I stop her to ask her a few questions. I explain that I'm writing a book about Iceland and am interested in her thoughts on some things, and does she have time? She says yes.

It turns out she's only sixteen. She's done with her compulsory schooling; she explains that in Iceland, you're required to go to school until you're sixteen. After that comes "upper secondary" school, for people ages sixteen to twenty. Beyond that is higher education, such as the University of Iceland, the University of Akureyri, the Agricultural University of Iceland, or a few others around the country. This young woman plans to go to Reykjavík in the fall, with hopes of studying law and languages. I ask her why; it's interesting to me that both Car Rental Guy and Café Girl want to be lawyers, and I wonder if this has to do with the economic crash and financial concerns.

For Café Girl, at least, the answer seems to be yes. She tells me of a friend of hers, also sixteen, who has to work twelve hours a day to help her family pay rent, since they lost so much in the crash. Café Girl doesn't want her own children to have those worries. She wants them to be able to just be kids when they are kids. Also, she watches people on TV law shows and she is impressed by the way they influence people, by the power they have. "They can tell you what you can and can't do," she says, "and they know all these words."

The day is cold, to me, but Café Girl is standing outside in a sleeveless top and doesn't seem to notice the chill. "Does it get cold here in winter?" I ask.

She smiles and says yes. I was expecting "Oh my gosh, it gets so cold!" but her definition of cold is likely different from mine. It seems last weekend was the weekend to be here; she says it was 20°C (about 70°F), gorgeous weather that happened to coincide with the town's annual "Mærudagar," or "Candy Days" festival.

Café Girl explains that during Candy Days, the town is separated into three sections: green, orange, and pink. Each section decorates profusely in its designated color, and people even dress themselves and their pets in the assigned color. The harbor is full of life with bands and dancing and festivities. Celebrations include beach volleyball, a market, a horse show, a ram show, and more.

We discuss the whale watching. "Húsavík lives on tourism in the summer," she explains, and depends on tourists going whale watching. If you're planning to go, she recommends going in the early morning on a sunny day.

I ask about Iceland and the studies that proclaim it to be the happiest nation in the world. "Icelandic people are happy," she says. "This is a beautiful country, and we are proud of it." Still, her wanderlust peeks through. She and a friend are already planning an escape, probably temporary, but who knows. They want to road trip across the U.S., or be exchange students in New Zealand.

I am conscious that Café Girl, while a delightful and friendly young woman, is also still working, and also can't be warm, no matter how used to the cold she is, so I thank her for her time and send her back inside. I have to say, I've been so charmed by everyone I've talked to so far. It can be hard for me, as something of an introvert, to strike up the conversations, but I'm curious to talk with people so whenever I can "screw my courage to the sticking place," as Shakespeare would say, I jump in. The Icelandic people, too, seem just as wary at first as I would be, but every one has been so kind and warm and interesting. I wish I were just slightly more outgoing, that I felt just a little more comfortable starting just a few more conversations, because these are my favorite parts of travel, the interactions with the people who live in a place. Making that connection is a huge part of creating a satisfying trip for me.

So, now, let me tell you why I am not going to go whale watching.

First, and perhaps least but not unimportant, is the time factor. It would take several hours, several cold wet hours, to go on a whale watching tour. However, if I really wanted to, I could have fit that in, so that's not the main reason.

Second, I've gone on a whale watching trip before, in Hawaii. Granted, the trips are undoubtedly very different, but the trip in Hawaii left us all scarred — literally. We went out on one of those Zodiac boats with the thick inflated rubber sides. There was only room for a few people to sit on the covered interior seats, so of course we young people left those seats for our elders. The rest of us were instructed to sit on the bouncy rubber sides, and hang on to one of the ropes wrapped around the inflated part. The boat tossed us around so much that our hands were rubbed raw. Rather than thinking, "Oh wow, this is amazing!" I simply was thinking, "Are we done yet? Are we done yet?" It was miserable. We did see humpback whales, and it was overwhelming, indescribable. But the whole trip left a bit of a bad taste in my mouth for whale watching. Some people on the trip still had scars on their knuckles a year later.

Third, while I'm guessing the trips out of Húsavík are on "normal" boats (and therefore we wouldn't be at risk of rubbing our knuckles raw again), I read a number of reports of whale watching, and many of them say things like, "We didn't see any whales, and half the people on the trip got sick."

And fourth, I'm not entirely sure how I feel about whale watching in general. Like I said, seeing a whale up close is an awe-inspiring experience. But I worry a bit about the impact all the trips have on the whales themselves. I've heard that an increase in whale watching tours can have an effect on the whales' feeding habits and their ability to rest. On occasion, boats collide with whales, causing them harm.

With all these in mind when I was planning my itinerary, I decided against a tour. However, Húsavík itself is fabulous, and I'm glad I stopped.

A quick left out of the parking lot and I'm back on Highway 85, which now curves up and over a bump in the land's edge. As I leave the town limits, on my right there are a couple mounds of grass that look suspiciously like completely turfed-over turf houses. Either that, or these particular mounds of grass are very house-shaped. Maybe elves live there. They have magical ways, I hear. Maybe they can make grass grow to look like a home.

Just before the road turns north again to skirt the northeast edge of the country, I turn off to Gljúfrastofa, the Visitor and Information Centre for Ásbyrgi Canyon. Ásbyrgi is a horseshoe-shaped canyon that is a part of the Vatnajökull National Park — yes, the same Vatnajökull National Park that includes Skaftafell and Svartifoss in the south. (Jökulsárlón sits outside Vatnajökull National Park, but just barely. If I'm reading the map right, Vatnajökull National Park has tremendously irregular boundaries, and not all areas included in the park seem to be contiguous. A somewhat Delaware-shaped chunk up here at Ásbyrgi, and continuing down to Dettifoss, is a part of the park, but there's a good bit of land around and below the area that is not.)

I stop at the visitor centre. Buoyed by my interesting chat with Café Girl, I am emboldened now to chat up Visitor Centre Guy and Visitor Centre Gal. Visitor Centre Guy is originally from Reykjavík; Visitor Centre Gal is from England. She has been working summers here for six years, but not too long ago found that her soulmate is a man from Iceland, so now she has moved to this chilly northern land.

We talk about how cold the day is, and again I comment how cold it must get in winter. Visitor Centre Gal tells me that actually, it feels colder in England in the winter than it does here. It's the geothermal heat, she says. In Iceland you pay for the maintenance of your heater, and then after that you can have all the heat you want, so people keep their homes nice and toasty. When you want to go outside, you go out and play, and then you come in and you're warm again in no time. In England, however, she says it's just cold, the wet kind of cold that seeps into your bones. And because people have to pay for their heat, houses are routinely colder due to money-consciousness.

I ask about the soil erosion I've learned about, and Visitor Centre Gal talks about the lupine, tells me about efforts being made now to remove or at least control the it. We discuss tourism, and Visitor Centre Guy agrees Iceland is reaching its limits on how many tourists it can handle at any one time. A common Icelandic sentiment, he says, is that the money is good but there are too many tourists.

Gljúfrastofa is a beautiful visitor centre, and many people have questions today for Visitor Centre Guy and Gal, so I thank them and move along to the canyon.

Geologically speaking, Ásbyrgi Canyon was probably formed by glacial flooding, but the legends say otherwise. According to the old Norse mythology, Odin's eight-legged horse Sleipnir stepped here and left his giant horseshoe-shaped footprint behind. The canyon is therefore nicknamed "Sleipnir's footprint." The legends do not address the question of where his other seven feet landed, and I guess that will have to remain a mystery. Legend also has it that this area is headquarters for the "hidden people" of Iceland ("huldufólk," a.k.a. elves), who live in the cracks and crevices of the cliffs.

Highway 861 has one purpose: to get visitors (and rangers/caretakers, too, I suppose) down to the canyon. The first thing I notice when I pull into the parking lot at the end of 861 is the trees. I've seen so few trees on this whole trip that I can't help but be a bit bewildered. My eyes drink in the sight of the woodlands. I park, and am thrown off by the fact that for the first time in a week, I can't see everything from here to the other side of Iceland. My view is blocked by this thin-trunked forest filled with birch and willow. Not sure where the path will take me, I follow directional signs that indicate a trail. I am amused by the sensation that I could almost get lost here, if I weren't careful. Not really; I'm in a canyon and eventually I'd find my way out. But having been able to see the steam of Blue Lagoon from five miles away, this is a nice change.

The trail leads through the lush canopy into the curve of the horseshoe. I see a branch of the trail leading off to the side, and next to it, a sign with a word in Icelandic. Intrigued, I follow the trail down to a little lake at the heel end of the canyon, and onto a wooden deck-like viewing platform from which I can look up the hundred-meter-high cliff walls. I feel surrounded by the peaceful, verdant beauty of the cliffs, the trees, and the lake. Another couple is just taking a picture of themselves, so I offer to take one of the both of them, and they return the favor for me. They leave, and I have this idyllic tranquility all to myself. I drink in the peace. I then notice a few more people on another viewing platform, to the west and higher up. "I wonder how they got there?" I say out loud, and head back to the original trail to see if I can find the platform. I do, easily. From this platform I get an even more expansive view, though I'll admit I liked the coziness of the lower platform. I realize that the trees and canyon are providing sanctuary from the ever-present wind. It is quiet here. The air seems cleaner. Trees at work. At Ásbyrgi, I breathe deeply.

I could stay here all day and soak in the soothing calm, but it's time to move on. Assuming that the trail I started out on is a giant

U, I continue in the direction I've been walking all along. Eventually, I start to wonder if I could, in fact, get lost here. Did I take a wrong turn? Shouldn't I be back to the parking lot by now? The trail started out wide and well traveled, but the path I'm on now feels like a secondary, unofficial path. I decide to trust it a while longer, and eventually I come out at the far west end of the parking lot. I see two tour buses have just arrived, and people are walking swiftly toward me. I realize I'm right by the toilets. I rush in ahead of the crowd. When I come out, there's a line.

I check my tires, and head on. Next stop, Dettifoss.

On my way back out 861, I'm reminded of Scotland again. In rural Scotland, there are a good number of one-lane roads. Not one lane each way, but just one lane, total. The way you maneuver them is that you watch out for cars coming your way. At intervals, there are wide spots labeled with a sign with a "P" in a blue box. Whoever is closer to the wide spot stops there and waits for the other car; if you're going to wait for the other person, you flash your lights so they know you've stopped, and that's how you pass. It's a smooth and efficient system, and everyone understands and uses it. Here on the 861, there are occasional wide spots with signs with an "M" in them rather than a "P," but they seem to be for the same purpose. However, the people driving here today, I'm assuming mostly tourists, seem to have no clue how to use these spots. When I see a car coming I head for an "M" spot to wait, but people coming in the other direction just stop where they are and wait for me. I'm not sure about the M spot thing, but it makes sense. If people know how to use it, that is.

My choices for driving south down to Dettifoss are Highway 862 and Highway 864. 862 is another road that is off-limits to non-4WD cars, though, so the 864 it is. This road is awful. Horrible. Terrible. (See more about this in the notes below.) By the time I drive the fifteen or so miles of gravel road to the Dettifoss pull-out, the weather has taken a turn for the worse and the drive has left me grumpy. But I'm here, so I park and zip my jacket up to my chin, wrap my hood around my ears against the unforgiving wind, and find the trail that leads down to the waterfall.

There are about a hundred rock steps at the start of the trail, and then there's a lava field to carefully pick my way through; people heading toward the waterfall seem to be walking more to the right, and people returning seem to be walking more to the left. There are no guardrails here, which feels both dangerous and exhilarating. The path leads me to the top of the waterfall, and I can literally walk right up to the falls — or even into it, if I wanted to. I creep closer and closer, carefully, though there's really no danger unless I actually step into the water. A mother is right at the water's edge, holding her toddler in her lap. Other people stand only a few feet from the water, which is rushing by with astonishing force. The spray from the falls curls up from the canyon forty-five meters below. I don't know if this is the most powerful of the waterfalls I've seen, or if it's just that I've never had the opportunity to get this close, but this is intense. I wonder if everyone else who stands here finds that they, too, can't help but think about what would happen if they walked into those waters. The power of these churning waters, flowing off the cliff to the river below, is mesmerizing.

Eventually I rip myself away from the force of the falls and head back up. Despite the difficult road, this parking lot is packed. I see a couple motorcyclists driving into the lot, and I imagine they must have had quite an unpleasant, bumpy ride.

I crawl along the road, continuing south on 864 another fifteen or twenty miserable miles, until eventually the road opens out back on my old friend, Highway 1, the Ring Road. Driving a paved road again is such a relief; it takes my body a while to calm down and stop jittering from the torture of 864. I only have two stops left, though: the geothermal area at Námafjall, and then I'm ending my day with a dip in the Mývatn Nature Baths. Relaxation, here I come!

The stretch of road between here and Námafjall (well, actually, between here and Akureyri) is the same route I drove in on two days ago. It's funny how quickly something can feel familiar, while at the same time there are always new things to notice. I see again some tall rock cairns I'd noticed before, running directly east-west. I looked those up the other day, and they are there from long ago, to help mark the route so people wouldn't get lost. I am again captivated by the various land formations leading into the Mývatn area. Finally, I'm again at the geothermal area of Hverir/Námafjall, but this time I pull in.

I find a parking spot at the front edge of the lot, right by the geothermal area. Stepping out of the car, my nose is immediately affronted by an assault of hot steamy sulfuric stench. Unpleasant, to say the least, but I know the nose adapts quickly so I wait it out, and soon it isn't nearly as offensive as that first whiff. (I also check my tires to see how they fared after the road to and from Dettifoss. Still round and inflated. Phew!)

The site is a light brown, mucky flat, completely barren, mottled here and there with boiling hot burbling gray-blue mudpools, most of which are roped off to keep people from walking into them or testing the waters, I assume. As I enter the field, a mother and son are exiting, plucking their feet off the ground with each step as though their shoes are stuck to the dirt. I immediately realize why. In some places, the clayey dirt is wet enough that I end up walking through a wide patch of muck. Luckily the top layer of mud is shallow; I don't sink in. Still, the soles of my shoes and slightly up the sides of the shoes are covered with the sticky clay.

I'm glad the rental car is not my own, and I marvel that it was as clean as it was when I got it. If other people who have rented that car have traveled the places I have, and the company has managed to keep the interior as clean as it was when I got it, they are doing a good job indeed.

None of these mudpools is the kind that erupts forcefully, but they do bubble and bloop and boil. They're actually quite beautiful, the contrast of light rusty brown with a gray-blue tinged with the slightest of greens. It's completely different from every other site I've been to in Iceland. Off to one side there's a stack of steaming rocks with people surrounding it. I believe, but am not certain, this is a fumarole, a crack in the Earth's crust, emitting steams and gasses. I am reminded again that this country is young, still constantly steaming and burping and shifting and growing.

My final stop for the day is the Mývatn Nature Baths, which I am visiting just for you, dear reader, so I can compare it with Blue Lagoon and report back. I know, I do make sacrifices. When I pull into the parking lot, it is completely packed. I think the parking spot I find is, in fact, the last spot available in the small lot. What's more, a tour group has just arrived before me, and there's a huge line and delay as I enter. Eventually, the people in the group are waved through, at which point … the person at the counter walks away. Um, okay? Maybe they want to allow time for that crowd to move through the dressing area, I think, so I stand patiently until finally someone comes to take my money. I've brought my own towel so I just pay for the right to enter the dressing room and get into the pool.

Although I wiped my shoes off as best as I could after Námafjall, they were still caked with mud. I suspect I'm not the only one nor the first; before you even go into the dressing rooms you're asked to take off your shoes and leave them under a bench or along a wall somewhere. Since this is Iceland, and theft is not really an issue, I'm not concerned.

As I make my way into the women's room, I wonder if it will be as lax as at Blue Lagoon. Before coming here I'd heard stories of people being yelled at for not properly washing their genitals, naked, before going into the numerous pools around the country. (Mostly I've heard stories of women being yelled at, actually. I guess maybe the men are washing their naked genitals thoroughly enough.) As I understand it, pools in Iceland don't use as many (or any?) chemicals as we do back in the states. Therefore, Icelanders are used to very thoroughly washing genitals, armpits, their heads, and their feet, before taking a public dip. From the tales I've heard, you can tell the Icelandic women from U.S. women by the fact the Icelandic women are walking around naked without care, whereas we U.S. ladies are all trying to cover up.

The dressing room is a madhouse, crowded with women from bench to bench, bare boobs and behinds and bathing suits. Much as I'd like to be carefree, I can't bring myself to let everything hang out in public. I wrap my towel around myself as best as I can before heading to the showers. At Blue Lagoon there were several shower stalls in which a person could have an illusion of privacy, until they were all in use anyway. Here, though, I don't see any private stalls. Just a long wall of showerheads. I wash, trying to be both thorough and quick, then slip on my swimming suit as fast as I can, and head out to the pool.

Baby, it is cold outside, and in the short walk from dressing room to pool I am blasted by the chill. I carefully walk down the ramp as quickly as I can, and maneuver myself to a shelf by a wall, where I can sit and soak. This time I have my hair up in a ponytail, out of the water; it took me two days to get Blue Lagoon fully washed out. As I sit and soak, with crowds of people around me talking in various tongues, I remember that I'm not really the bath-taking type. I've never really found the charm in lying in a vat of water. I get fidgety. Even here, that starts to happen. What I'd imagined would be peaceful and restorative is actually sort of weird, like taking a bath with a bunch of people I don't know. A man and woman paddle over to the empty spot next to me and start making sexy sounding noises. Another man, having not seen the ramp he was supposed to walk down, tries to get in the pool right across from me, and instantly slips on the very slick ground beneath the water. I don't see him fall, but I hear it. He proclaims something in another language. I have a feeling I know approximately what he said.

So I close my eyes and pretend no one else is there, but the couple next to me are still sexy-talking, and the water makes them sound even closer to me than they are. As far as I can see, the whole pool is crowded. There seems to be an open area out to my left, but I can't figure out how to get there.

"I am relaxing," I tell myself. "This is really, really relaxing. An ultimate relaxing cultural experience. I am so relaxed!"

But I can't fool myself. The part of me that just doesn't really "get" baths in general, wins. After a short while, I doggy-paddle back to the ramp, head inside to wash my privates in public again, get dressed, and head on back to Akureyri.

The cliff-side road into town is not nearly as daunting as it was the last time I drove in, so I realize I must have been severely tired when I first drove it. This time, I know where the pull-outs are, so when I see a giant cruise ship in the harbor, nearly as large as the whole town of Akureyri itself, I am able to pull over and get a picture. Several other people do the same. The ship is gigantic, like it might be a bath toy for Odin's eight-legged horse, the one big enough to have left a footprint the size of Ásbyrgi Canyon.

Arriving back in town, the first thing I do is fill up the car with gas. See? I can still learn.

Back at the apartment, I peek into the laundry room to see if the washer is available. I don't want to carry around a dirty and wet swimsuit and towel for another week. Surprise! The washer is available! I put my clothes in, and … wait a minute. The washer says "system error." It's Sunday, there's no one in the office. I start pushing buttons, and somehow get to a screen where it asks me to select the language I want the directions to be shown in. I try to scroll down to "English" but the screen won't scroll. I take my clothes out of the machine, and … wait. The machine seems to be working now. Except I apparently have changed the language to what I think might be Czech. Well, I've done laundry here before, maybe I can remember enough about what buttons to push? And, sure enough, the machine lets me start my wash, in Czech. Whatever I did, it's working! I am a Washing Machine Ninja.

Tomorrow, I leave Akureyri already. This trip is flying by.

If I came back with a 4WD vehicle:

Some of the sites I wanted to visit are only accessible via 862, the road out by Ásbyrgi that I couldn't drive. For example, there's the Jökulsárgljúfur Canyon, within the Jökulsárgljúfur National Park area — which is now part of the Vatnajökull National Park. It's said to be one of the most impressive of Iceland's river canyons, and some of the waterfalls and land formations look spectacular. Within the same area is Hljóðaklettar, the "whispering cliffs" or "echo cliffs." Visitor Centre Gal said it's called the echo canyon not because your voice echoes, but because when you're there, sound reverberates and "you don't know where the river is … unless you know where the river is."

A note about roads:

I have a wee little beef here, a bone to pick with Icelandic Tourism. Let's take a few minutes to talk about the road to Dettifoss, and the Diamond Circle road. Here I'm going to have to refer to information I didn't have until five days after I drove the Diamond Circle, so please forgive the break in narrative.

As mentioned previously, after Húsavík, I headed east along Highway 85 to continue along the Diamond Circle. The point of a circle is that it is a circle, right? Meaning you go in one direction without backtracking. So I continued along Highway 85, with my next destination of Ásbyrgi in mind. Before heading down to Ásbyrgi, I stopped in at Gljúfrastofa, the Visitor and Information Centre where I met Visitor Centre Guy and Gal.

Car Rental Guy had warned me that one of the roads, 862 or 864, was not good to get to Dettifoss, but he couldn't remember which, so he said to talk to the people in the area, as they would know. Car Rental Guy was right once again. Visitor Centre Guy told me 862 — very important, this is coming FROM THE NORTH, from Highway 85 — 862 is a far worse road, suitable really only for 4WD (if I'd driven my rental car on it, my contract would have been void), and said that I should take 864 south. So I went south on 864, and endured sixteen miles of severely potholed gravel roads. "Endured" is perhaps not the right word. "Cursed" is more accurate. I don't remember how long it took to drive that sixteen miles, but I was going somewhere between fifteen and twenty-five miles per hour most of the way. It was awful. (I've read descriptions of the road as "washboards," and I don't know if that's a common term for a road, but it definitely describes the 864 — you feel like you're driving on a washboard.)

To finish my loop — since again, this is a circle — I then continued south on 864, another twenty miles of potholed, washboard, gravel road. The majority of this road was actually not quite as bad as the northern portion had been (relatively speaking that is; it was still an awful road). In fact, at one point, I noted that the road south from Dettifoss was one of the few places in Iceland, outside of cities, where the road was at level with its surroundings, where I wasn't in constant danger of driving off the side and flipping my car into the vast Icelandic barrenness. It was a relief. That is, until I reached the final mile. With just about 5000 feet to go to get back to the Ring Road, 864 became the worst road I have ever been on. No road, really; just nothing but washboard. At one point I slowed down to seven miles per hour and still was worried that my car (and myself) would be rattled into a million pieces. Finally, just a few feet before Highway 1, the road flattened out a bit more, and my teeth stopped chattering. I peeled my hands from the steering wheel, stretched, took a deep breath, and continued on my way.

Here's the thing, though. When I interviewed the mayor of Akureyri five days later, I talked a bit about the Diamond Circle and the marketing push to bring people to the area, and told him I had not been too excited about driving on 864. He told me the road to Dettifoss is wonderful, if you drive north UP the 862 from Highway 1. (862 will take you to the west side of the falls; 864 takes you to the east side. Go online if you'd like to read debate over which has the best views, if that's a concern.)

But the problem with that is, as I mentioned, this is a CIRCLE. If Iceland and the people promoting the Diamond Circle want me to drive the route in a circle, then I'm not sure how I'm to do it without driving 864. There are no other roads in the area, and even if I had 4WD, Visitor Centre Guy told me the northern part of 862 is horrendous. (I've since read that there are plans to improve the rest of 862, north from Dettifoss, but there's no timeline on this.) In theory I could make a giant loop on the 85 out to the east, but that would add three hours to the trip at a minimum. So, if they want me to experience the Diamond Circle, at this point that means they're asking me to drive 864, and I have to say that I can't in good conscience recommend that to anyone; at least, not without a warning to be prepared. I'm sure some people won't mind the ride, but some will, and I'm guessing the smaller your car the more you'll feel the road. Since travelers often get the smallest car possible to save money, this could be you. If you plan to drive 864, know that it is going to shake the fillings out of your teeth, and hopefully you won't puncture a tire on a rock. And do not drive this road without gravel insurance!

One last note: If the road to/from Dettifoss on 864 is suitable for 2WD, trust me, stay off the roads that are not suitable for 2WD! I can't even imagine!

So that's my commentary on the road to Dettifoss. I'll have more to say about Iceland's infrastructure at the end of the book.

Akureyri to Hellissandur

Monday, August 5, 2013

The sun rose in Akureyri at 4:17 a.m. today, but I can tell you from having witnessed it that the sky started to get light much earlier. I'm not sure it ever gets fully dark. Every time I wake up it's at the very least a little light. Sometime after 2:00 I woke up and looked out. It was dark, but I could still see the shadows of the glaciers. As a person whose sleep is highly influence by the sunrise, I am grateful once again for the blackout curtains.

At any rate, the day has risen with the promise of sunshine, a welcome relief after two days of overcast skies and misty rain. I'm running a little behind; I'd hoped to get out the door by 8:00, but am not ready until 8:30. Nonetheless, I drop off my key in the key box and head out into the day, full of optimism and joy. I'm feeling that freedom of being one week into a vacation — it always takes a week, doesn't it, to really relax? Like when you get a massage (at, for example, Blue Lagoon), and the masseuse rubs your right shoulder and it hurrrrts, but you think, don't fight it, sink into it, release the tension. And finally you do, and it doesn't hurt anymore. Vacation is like that. The first week, I can't get all the cares of everyday out of my mind. But finally, about a week in, I start to breathe again.

And so, I am breathing again, and thinking about life, and falling in love with northwest Iceland (what is it about the northwest part of a country that it is always the best part? Am I right, Washington?), and falling in love with a new little remote town, and all is well in the world!

Until …

The Gravel Road.

But let's start at the very beginning.

Packing. The problem with packing efficiently is that because you've utilized every possible millimeter of space, you have to pack efficiently every time you repack your suitcase. There isn't room to just throw things in. Items must be arranged and tucked and managed. Last night, I thought, "Oh, I can pack in the morning." This morning, I wish I'd done it last night. But it gets done. I double- and triple-check the room and head out. It's always strange, seeing a room that for a short time was home revert back to empty and generic once all my belongings are back in my bags. It's just another room again. Lifeless, no longer mine. Nothing but a memory.

Door locked, key dropped off, I'm on my way. According to Google, my route will take about five hours and forty-five minutes. Another long driving day, but tomorrow will be short. I set my GPS for my first stop, Skagaströnd, where there's an old-school country-and-western radio station and museum, and I hear the owner is a singer who takes requests. I've read there's also a Museum of Prophecies in town. I am off to dance to some home-grown music, then get my fortune told, according to the old legends.

The drive from Akureyri to Skagaströnd is just over a hundred miles, which gives me plenty of time to think. This is a new thing, I realize; up until today I've been tense driving the narrow roads. Are the roads west out of Akureyri wider, or am I finally more comfortable with them? I suspect it's a bit of both. Either way, my mind starts to wander.

Once again, I am in love with driving in the morning. The gargantuan tour buses with their giant one-eyed window panes, designed to allow maximum viewing by the passengers, haven't started rattling down the roads yet. In fact, almost no one has. I'm not counting cars-per-minute today, because there are so few. Iceland is mine alone.

I start thinking about what it is about tour buses that I so dislike.

To begin, I want to make it clear: If tour buses are your thing, I don't have a problem with that. Enjoy your travel however you enjoy it. To each his own. The buses certainly have their advantages — no stressful driving or chip-and-PIN gas stations, convenient access, the opportunity to meet and mingle with other people. Tour buses are not a match for me, though. Why is that, exactly?

After some pondering, I decided it has to do with what I want out of a country. Tour buses will offer you The Best Of a country — the highlights, the prettiest, most powerful, most impressive. (And, to an extent, the most convenient for the buses to get to.) If travel is a relationship, then tour buses are a first date. It's where you see only the side of the country it wants you to see. The country, all dressed up, on its best behavior; the glamorous, glittering side. Best foot forward. Do the fun things. Show you what they think you want to see.

And that's fine. There's nothing wrong with first dates. After all, you can't get to the second date without the first, right? But I don't want to see The Best Of a country. I want to see its Soul. I want to see its Heart. I want a deeper relationship that shows me who a country really is, and for that, you have to get off the tour bus.

That never-ending drone of a drive around the east coast of Iceland, that's the friend who talks too much, but who, if you listen, always shares nuggets of beauty, and you love her through it all because of who she is. The early morning Iceland that I love, that's the intimate wake-up time with your soulmate; that's sharing the lazy, cozy, slightly disheveled but still magical moments of togetherness, the secret moments that no one else is privileged to see. Finding unexpected places is finding the quirky parts of a new friend that surprise and delight you.

Even the run-down places of a country, these places are the scars of past hopes and broken dreams; these tell you the history of hope in a country. Because humans never build without hope. I see ruins and I want to know, Who built this? Why did they build it? Why did they build it here? Every structure holds the story of someone's dream. At the very least, someone built with hopes others would follow. At most, they built with the hopes of not just building a place, but also building a life, building safety and love and memories.

And the land itself, in this land where the stories are far older than the buildings, the land formations here tell the stories and history of the country, of the forces that shaped it, maybe long gone now but still evident in the earth itself. If you're paying attention you'll suddenly find yourself in an area bursting with bright magenta wildflowers, or by a field covered with shallow, milky-green pools, such as I drive by today. I am driving along, vaguely noticing the broad valley filled with water to my left. The road gathers closer to one of the pools and I suddenly realize it's not clear or blue but rather a milky green like Lake Lagarfljót, in the way Blue Lagoon and the Mývatn pools are a rich milky blue. It's just a brief moment, and of course there's no way to stop and take a picture. So I savor it and am grateful to Iceland for sharing with me this fleeting treasure.

Only when you pay attention to a country will it start to reveal its secrets. These are the parts of a country I want to know. The mysteries, the memories, the hopes, the dreams, the hidden secrets, the quiet moments. This tells you far more about a country than The Best Of ever could.

And so. Tour buses. They're good for many things (especially smaller vans; don't forget there are tours of all sizes); you have an instant connection with other travelers, and you know you won't get lost. But as I go along this journey, more and more I think Iceland is a land best discovered intimately, in small doses; and quietly, in solitude or at least with room to breathe. If you're coming to Iceland, I encourage you to find a way to find one place that you can claim as your own for even a small window of time; one place that will lead you to the kinds of discoveries I think people come to Iceland for. If you come all this distance, it can't hurt to step off the beaten path, at least a little, right?

With the very important caveat, if you were going to take the "off the beaten path" thing literally, that off-road driving is illegal. The other day, in the south, I was driving by one of those barren areas with the green fire extinguisher foam-like coating. I could see that at some point, someone drove off the road and destroyed the tenuous growth. The tire trails leading off into the distance had killed all the foliage in their path and left behind glaring scars on the land. Iceland's topography is beautiful, but also quite fragile in places. It takes careful, thoughtful visitors to help ensure it stays that way.

And so with these thoughts in mind, I traverse the globe from Akureyri, weaving south and west and occasionally north, through vast isolated fields, surprised but delighted to find little towns that come out of nowhere. These towns are all somehow so inviting; I want to stop and visit every one and stay a week and become a part of the community. I pass by one named Varmahlíð, tucked in amidst the rivers and the more hilly/mountainous terrain I'm passing by. I'd say I can't very well judge Iceland's east, as it didn't have the chance to show me its best side. The south of Iceland was simply breathtaking, indescribable in its beauty. But this northwest, here I'm finding a sort of pastoral tranquility. A beauty that is both unassuming and peaceful; a landscape that is a bit more mellowed and mature than that of other parts of the country. Earlier, I described parts of the south as the Earth in a moody adolescent form; up here, it feels like a land with some wisdom to share, for whoever might be listening. On another visit, I'd definitely make more time for the northwest.

Soaking in the many subtle wonders of this landscape, I continue on past Varmahlíð until I reach the bay of Húnaflói, at which point I head north toward Skagaströnd. Interestingly, in this remote reach, I encounter only the second police car I've seen since I've been here; the other, of course, was at Akureyri, the one that returned time and again to watch me standing at the steps of City Hall while I waited for the mayor in vain. This police car, unconcerned about my going 80 kph in a 90 kph zone, takes a right to head north on the 745, toward the north end of the peninsula and whatever trouble lurks there.

I am on the top of the world. The sun is shining brightly and the bay — is it the Greenland Sea yet at this point? — is a stunning blue. All over the country, it is harvest time, and farmers have gathered up their hay and baled it into hay-bale shaped bags, mostly white but occasionally blue, light green, black. These bales dot the countryside, testimonial to the labors of the land, the breath of the country. It is beautiful. This sun-drenched day, the bright bales of hay, the deep blue of the sea, the horses and sheep in the country-side, it was all made for me and I feel amazing.

Finally, a short jaunt of gravel road behind me — nothing I can't handle — I reach Skagaströnd, and I am instantly in love. It is perfect in the way Icelandic towns are perfect: crisp, clean, a smattering of colorful houses, a glistening waterfront. I could move here. I know nothing about it but it welcomes me home.

Except, everything is closed. Everything but the gas station, it seems. I go inside the gas station store to ask about the Museum of Prophecies, and while I'm there it seems every man in town must be coming by to greet the store owner and each other, check in on the happenings of the day, find out the news.

The news, it turns out, is that it's a bank holiday. Is the Museum of Prophesies open? No. It's not open today, and it's not normally open on Mondays anyway. The store owner points to a poster in the window. It is apparently the poster for the Museum, only it's in Icelandic. Of course. Why it didn't occur to me that it might be a good idea to figure out and write down the Icelandic for "Museum of Prophesies" — or whatever its real name might be — is beyond me. This isn't my first time in a country where English isn't the first language, but most of my traveling has been in such countries. I'm realizing I'm going to have to do a little more homework on future trips when I can't speak the native tongue.

Regardless, this town is gorgeous. I imagine myself coming here, inviting a group of friends to rent a house and stay here a week. Granted, it's sunny today, and everything feels perfect in Iceland when it's sunny. If I were here in a downpour, my opinion could be different. If you'd asked me if my travel moods were tied to weather moods, I'd have said no, but I'm starting to realize I'm more fickle than I would have liked to admit. Regardless, this little fishing village, with its waterfront statue of a phoenix rising out of … used car parts?, and its boat-filled harbor, and its white houses with multi-colored roofs — a tan house with a green roof, a red house with a white roof — with its country-and-western museum and its water cooler gas station store, and its closed-on-Mondays museum where I certainly would have learned the truth about what my future holds, reminds me that taking the time to go out of my way when I travel often pays off in spades. Skagaströnd is not on the Ring Road; I had to go a few dozen miles off the highway to get here, but here I've found a little haven of bliss.

I head back south, through Blönduós, where I stop briefly to admire the town. I drive toward the edge of town to get a look where the river through Blönduós opens out into Húnafjörður, the fjord, and stop to take a video of the scene. I step out, and immediately halt in my tracks: There are sheep droppings everywhere. EVERYWHERE. I look around to see if there are sheep anywhere, but there are none. Maybe I've misidentified the droppings? I haven't really made a study of droppings previously, but here in Iceland, it seems maybe I should. Something has dropped here, all over, and I tread gingerly while I make the video. I re-think my previous idea of coming to stay in Blönduós; now, I think, I might come to Blönduós, but stay somewhere where there aren't droppings all over. Small detail.

Back on Highway 1, my southward trek eventually bears east again. I have read that there are "three countless things" in Iceland. The first, the lakes of Arnarvatnsheidi moor. The second, the islands of Breiðafjordur. And the third, the hills of Vatnsdalur, a.k.a. the Vatnsdalshólar. The lakes are apparently in the highlands, where I won't be going anytime soon without 4WD. The islands will be on my right as I drive out the Snæfellsnes peninsula today. But the third, the hills of Vatnsdalur, these are next on my itinerary. I have written in my notes that they'll be about twenty kilometers after Blönduós, so I make mental note of my mileage (or kilometerage) and continue south.

Again, as with so many things, I need not have worried that I would miss them. These small hills, mostly pyramid shaped (and, interestingly, the site of the last execution in Iceland, in 1830), are indeed innumerable. I stop at a picnic spot to absorb the variety of hills, their shapes and colors and sizes. For a long time, their origin was uncertain, but from what I read there is now consensus that these hills are the result of a giant landslide off Vatnsdalsfjall (a mountain), long before Iceland was settled. Strange formations, indeed. It seems almost impossible that these are a natural result of anything. Surely the hidden people have built all these mounds, surreptitiously, at night when no one is looking. Has anyone dug inside the hills? Do we know for certain these aren't all just homes to countless elves? Or perhaps the leftover dwellings from an elf convention? My mind can't help but start to make up stories here, in this wondrous place that must spark countless imaginations.

I'm back on the Ring Road, still weaving elf tales in my head, when it happens.

I hit The Gravel Road.

After the Dettifoss debacle, I would have been happy never to drive on gravel road again. But here I am, and my GPS very definitely is telling me to turn off onto Highway 59, which very definitely is gravel. Hoping it won't last too long, I slow down and drive.

It lasts. It lasts a very long time. I drive along carefully, as these roads are still narrow and raised, but now with the added danger of being gravel. There are not a lot of other cars here, but when they rush up behind me, I edge as far to the right as I can, and signal for them to pass. I moderate my speed carefully, knowing that if I pop a tire out here on a sharp rock or a deep pothole, I would be hiking a very long way to get help. My one thought is to wonder how long this will last. All the way out to Hellissandur, where I'm spending the night? That's more than a hundred fifty miles away. Surely it can't be. Surely not.

Off to my left, as I'm crossing a short bridge, I see a crevice, a canyon, hidden, tucked away, as though I'm not supposed to see it, not supposed to know it's there. Just past the bridge I see another car parked on the side of the road in a pull-out, so I veer off slowly to join them. I walk to the crevice, and it's beautiful, the waters pure Icelandic crystal clear, the bright green foliage creeping down the sides of the rocks to reach the water below. And then, I hear … rushing water. Yes, there is definitely a waterfall somewhere nearby. Following my ears, I walk a safe distance from the edge of the crevice until I see the source of the sound. A little, secret, hidden waterfall, small and multi-tiered. Noting the level of the water where I am, and knowing how far below the surface the river is a little farther down, I know there must be a good-sized drop somewhere, but I can't see it without getting closer to the edge of the crevice than I'm comfortable with. I've read about getting too close to the edge; you never know when a cliff will decide it's time to erode. So I stay back. Still, what I can see is beautiful. Like the waterfall at the top of Highway 939, this seems to have been placed here just for me, a reward for the miles of gravel road I've endured. You can't see this waterfall from the road, and wouldn't know it was here if you weren't walking by. I wonder how many people have driven by without even knowing it exists.

Walking back to my car, I realize I wandered farther than I thought, and I hadn't paid attention while I was following the sound of the waterfall. I've lost my bearings a bit, and I can't see my car. This is wide open land. Getting lost out here would not be a good idea. I'm a bit downhill, so I aim myself "up." After a while,

I'm back at road level. I've roamed a ways west of my car, but at least it's in sight again. Note to self: Keep track of where you are.

The gravel road continues. On and on and on. And on. And on. A nearly full bottle of water sits on the passenger seat beside me, tempting me. My throat is parched, but I have a suspicion there is no restroom around for hours, so the bottle remains closed. I'm very glad to have gassed up the car when I did; I have plenty of gas but wouldn't hope for a gas station out here, either. Or food. Or anything. I see houses occasionally, and wonder what it would be like to live so far away from everything. You'd have to be self-sufficient, certainly. I imagine I'd find myself out here filling potholes on occasion, just to make my own trip into town smoother. It seems no one out here thinks that, though, as the road is quite rough. Not Dettifoss rough, but rough still the same.

And then, at last! I'm on paved road! Hallelujah! The last bit of Highway 59 is paved road, and I turn off, west on 54, and it's paved too. It's …

Oh. It's short-lived, is what it is. Gravel road again.

But now, I think I'm finally officially on the Snæfellsnes peninsula. My destination is … well, it's not near. It seems very far away, in fact, and though I haven't had a drink of water for an hour, I wasn't so careful with my water intake at the start of my day. I'm starting to look at the rocks on the side of the road and evaluate how well they would block me from the view of any passing traffic.

The road may be abominable, but the landscape is incredible, breathtaking. I have to keep reminding myself to keep my eyes on the road, because the deep, bright cerulean blue of the fjord that is now on my right, Hvammsfjörður, is incredible. What's more, in contrast to the vast majority of Iceland's rural houses which have either white walls and red roofs or occasionally white walls with green or light blue roofs, here there are houses with white walls and crisp blue roofs that match the astonishing color of the fjord. More than ever, I feel thwarted by the fact there's nowhere to stop; I want to capture one of these blue-and-white houses against the twin blue backdrop of the water. But, the road is curving around enough that if I parked on the road, cars coming from either direction might not see me in time to stop. I imprint the images on my mind instead, and try to keep my eyes on the road.

Finally, I reach a pull-out at a point that overlooks the water and the islands of the fjord. I'm not sure where I am, but I speculate that I might be looking out over the countless islands of Breiðafjordur, or at least some of the outliers; I'm not sure where one fjord begins and another ends. The islands are indeed countless; most of them are uninhabited, but a few are dotted with houses. One seems to have a larger settlement, with several buildings. The water glistens in the sun. I take dozens of pictures, trying to capture in a photo what my eyes are seeing, but it's impossible. To be believed, this vista must be seen in person.

I'm not alone here. The breathtaking view is enough to stop anyone in their tracks as they drive by. Though it didn't seem like there were so many cars on the road, there's a now steady stream of people stopping, taking in the view, and driving off again. Most speak in hushed tones, awed by the sight, taking in this unbelievable beauty. This view, this is the ultimate reward for going off the paved road. This is extraordinary.

This is Iceland.

Mercifully, the gravel road eventually ends. At the T in the road where gravel road meets paved road, the paved road in one direction leads to Stykkishólmur, where I'd read there's a lighthouse, and in the other direction to Hellissandur, my final destination for the day. I'd planned to go to Stykkishólmur but can't bear the possibility of running into more gravel road. All told, I estimate I've traveled more than eighty kilometers of gravel road today, and my nerves are shattered. I take the road to the left — the glorious, paved road — on to Hellissandur.

Out here, free at last from the stress of the gravel road, I am finally able to appreciate the beauty of this peninsula. It occurs to me that there must be — must be — another way to get out here; another *paved* way. I know tour buses come out here every day, and while one "extreme" van did whip by me at one point (traveling at a rather unsafe speed, if you ask me), that was the only bus I saw. How did I miss the paved road? Where was the paved road? I am obsessively jealous of people who didn't have to endure the gravel road, but then I remind myself that none of them saw that transcendent view of the fjord. And I think, yes, Iceland has its problems with infrastructures and roads, but if the road to that spot were paved, it would be swarming with people, and the peace of the place would be lost. There are tradeoffs. It isn't always obvious what is right or best.

The landscape of the Snæfellsnes peninsula is inspiring. Not just to me, apparently, but also to those who wrote Iceland's sagas. As I come to an inlet, I see a picnic spot with a placard of some sort. I park and investigate. The sign welcomes me to Eyrbygg-ja, the settlement of Eyrarsveit. The people who once lived at Eyri were called the Eyrbyggjar, says the sign. I get confused that there seem to be so many place names for the same thing, though I'm sure if I knew the language it would all make sense. A second part of the sign declares that in 1813, Sir Walter Scott declared, "Of all the various records of Icelandic history and literature, there is none more interesting than Eyrbyggja Saga," and maps out where on the peninsula the various parts of the saga took place. A third sign indicates that Viking ruins can still be seen at Öndverðareyri.

Also, according to one sign, there used to be a leprosy hospital out here. Which seems like an odd place for a leprosy hospital, as well as a strange thing to put on the sign about the saga. But at least it's pretty.

Around 3:30 or 4:00, I see some tour buses, I assume heading back to Reykjavík. I don't know where they came from, and I don't know where they've been, but I knew they'd be here, with their secret knowledge of the coveted secret paved roads.

Following speed limit signs, I slow considerably to a near crawl as I drive through Grundarfjörður. This small town of about a thousand people is so cute it almost pains me to keep driving. I hope my own destination, not far away now, will be this cute. I can see a couple different cafés and restaurants, B&Bs, people walking about all over town. I imagine this is a popular spot for people to stay, if they are familiar with the area. I know I looked at a couple B&Bs here, but they were all completely full, and besides which, I didn't know until now that I really wanted to stay here. At the west end of the town, a mountain, Kirkjufell, juts magnificently out of the water, protecting the town in its shadow and making for a stunning setting.

I continue on, past the larger town of Ólafsvík and its space-age-inspired church (making note of a gas station and what seems to be a grocery store), past the small village of Rif, and then finally, I am at Hellissandur. My GPS is telling me where to turn, but I can see my Hotel, the Hotel Hellissandur, on the right, across the street from a gas station, much to my joy. To my left, Snæfellsjökull, a grand volcano with a glacier on top, stands bright and white and grand in the sunshine, congratulating me on reaching my destination.

I am here, at the western edge of Iceland, for two nights. On check-in, the woman at the front desk asks me if I want to make a reservation for dinner. I remember the last time this happened, in

Vík, when the charming Front Desk Guy charmed me into paying $45 for some raw horse meat. "Is it expensive?" I ask, "Or are there cheaper things on the menu?"

"It's not all expensive," she says. "There are less expensive things."

I decide to go ahead and make a reservation for 6:30, then head up to my room. It's just after 5:00 now. Not that this is the most important thing, but I can't get my phone or computer to connect to the WiFi, and I was promised WiFi. Each day when I get to where I'm going, I've been checking in with home via Whatsapp, to let them know all is still well. I like my WiFi. I know you understand. I go down to the front desk, where the front desk woman explains they've been having trouble with WiFi upstairs for "the last few days." I am suspicious. Do they tell everyone that? If I came again in a year, would I hear that they've been having trouble for "the last few days"? She tells me there's WiFi in the lobby, which explains the teenage boy sitting here with his phone, next to his father with his iPad. I, too, am able to connect here. I carefully carry my phone, now hooked into WiFi, up to my room, as though the WiFi is water I'm carrying in a very full cup, and if I carry it steadily enough I'll be able to bring the full glass into my room. As if the WiFi is a soap bubble I'm precariously maneuvering through space, hoping it hasn't popped by the time my room door shuts behind me. As though the connection in one area is a thread that can be pulled, like taffy, into another area.

But it does work.

The WiFi cuts in and out on both computer and phone, but at least I have a connection. I upload a video for friends back home, and it takes more than half an hour. By the time it's done, it's time for dinner.

As I suspected, I didn't really need a reservation. The dining room is all but empty. I pick a table on the side, out of direct sunlight but with a good view of the glacier.

The waitress is one of the first people I've met whose English isn't nearly perfect. I can't tell accents, so I don't know if hers is Icelandic or something else. Regardless, she's lovely and sweet. She offers me a menu and asks if I'd like anything to drink.

"Do you have a lemon drop?" I ask, with great hope. I could do with a lemon drop.

She gives me a nervous, apologetic blank stare.

"Or a Long Island?"

"That's ice tea, right?" she says.

"Well, I mean, it's alcoholic."

"I'll check."

She goes to check, and I wait. The cost of alcohol is a bit prohibitive, prohibitive enough that I haven't had a drink since I've been here, and I don't really need the drink. It just sounds nice about now, after ten million miles of driving on the top of the world.

She returns. "No, I'm very sorry, we don't have either of these."

Sigh. I'll just have water. I order the cheapest thing on the menu, a hamburger. When it comes, it's like a parallel universe hamburger, where it's similar but just a bit off. Instead of pickles, for example, they've put slices of cucumber inside. But it's tasty enough. I sit and write and eat, drink my water. The father and son have moved themselves and their gadgets from the lobby to the dining room, but they are still there, fiddling away on phone and iPad. Another couple is goo-goo eyeing each other off to the side. It's nearly 7:00, but I'm farther west and the daylight will last even longer out here. Sunset will be nearly half an hour later here than in Akureyri, not until 10:42 tonight.

After dinner, I ask at the front desk for the best route down to the beach. "If you walk this way," the woman tells me, pointing at the map, "there is a very nice spot with a bench where you can sit and look."

So after washing up and grabbing my camera, I walk to the bench and sit and look, and think about being at the edge of Iceland. I've driven almost the whole way around this cold, dramatic, extraordinary island. In two days, I'll be back in Reykjavík. Have I gotten out of this journey what I wanted?

A thought I'd had earlier in the day returns to me. Coming here, I think I planned to have an epiphany. It was never a fully formed idea. I realize, though, that in the back of my mind, I expected to come away Changed. Somehow. What change, I don't know. What needed to be changed, I don't know. Why I thought Iceland would change me, I don't know. Maybe it's the magical mysticalness of Iceland, the fact that it's always been so far away and out there, that it must somehow carry with it Answers and Wisdom. But did I get Answers? Did I get Wisdom? Did I even stop to ask Questions?

I don't know.

Walking back, I wonder if Monday is laundry day; so many houses have laundry hanging out to dry in the sun on multitudes of clotheslines. As I walk, I watch a woman take her sheets down off the clothes line, take them inside, then come back out to head off on a walk, bopping to a tune on her iPod. I hear children playing down the street. A couple is out for a stroll. For a town of just over five hundred, there's a lot going on.

Back up in my room, I watch the goings-on continue outside my window. A trio are walking down the road now, their advancement announced by their super-elongated shadows. The evening sun has stretched these shadows diagonally across two lanes of traffic and the length of another lane beyond that. The shadows bob and waver as the people attached to their feet walk in the never-ending sunset.

A cat across the street sits and stares at unseen beings, maybe the hidden people. It occurs to me that I've seen very few pets. I know that dogs used to be banned in Reykjavík, but I don't know anything about cats. Seeing one makes me smile.

The sun will go to bed far later than I will tonight. I'm exhausted. Shortly after 9:00, I pull closed the blackout curtains (two layers of curtains here, and the blackout curtains are very efficient). I try to read a bit from Game of Thrones, but my eyes won't stay open.

Next time:

I hate to admit it, but before coming to Iceland I knew absolutely nothing about the entire Skagafjörður region, including Varmahlíð and much more. Although only about one hundred and forty people live in Varmahlíð, there are six — six! — places of accommodation in the area, including three in town and another three within about twenty kilometers. The Glaumbær Museum has preserved turf-roofed buildings from the eighteenth century, where you can see what life in those times was like; pictures I've seen online make me wish I'd known about it so I could have stopped. The town is also home to Karlakórinn Heimir, one of Iceland's most famous men's choirs, and Miðgarður, a community center/concert hall where they perform. The region is highly agricultural, with lots of the famous Icelandic horses, and also several river-rafting outfits. Check before you come — it looks like much of this is only open/available during the summer months — but it definitely seems worth a visit. In fact, all the towns and villages in northwest Iceland look tremendously inviting. I think there's far more to see and do here than I ever realized.

If you are particularly interested in horses, and plan to be traveling this area around September, do some research about "Skrapatungurétt." This is an annual round-up of horses in the Laxárdalur Valley in northwest Iceland. As I understand it, the horses run wild in the highlands and valleys over the summer, and Skrapatungurétt is apparently the time when farmers gather to bring the horses home. There is, I've read, an accompanying community celebration ball at Blönduós, which I can only imagine would be fabulous fun (watch your step). That's about all I know about Skrapatungurétt — but as I said, if it sounds interesting to you, I would think it would be an amazing experience.

Incidentally, the country-and-western radio station out of Skagaströnd is on the dial at FM 96.7 and 100.76. The Museum of Prophesies is named Spákonuhof. It's closed on Mondays.

As far as gravel roads, it's actually not that hard to know where they are so as not to be surprised by them. I become too dependent on my GPS, and didn't spend enough time looking at actual maps. Now that I know what I know, it looks like on many maps the gravel roads are brown, and the paved roads are red. If I'd been paying more attention, I could have known this in advance!

If you want to read the Eyrbyggja saga, or "Saga of the Ere-Dwellers," go to http://sagadb.org/eyrbyggja_saga.en.

Snæfellsnes Peninsula

Tuesday, August 6, 2013

"Descend, bold traveler, into the crater…"

Did you know that in Jules Verne's *Journey to the Center of the Earth*, the entrance to the center of the Earth is at Snæfellsjökull? I did not know this before coming here, but I know this now. Snæfellsjökull is actually a mountain named Snæfell, but there are two other mountains in Iceland named Snæfell (as well as one on the Isle of Man, technically Snaefell), so this one is called Snæfellsjökull, to "avoid confusion."

That's the thing about Icelandic place names. For whatever reason, there are lots of places with similar or the same names, and I think the primary reason is so if you're using your GPS and you never give your GPS a proper name like "Mr. SmartyGPS" or "Ms. Getsyouthere" or "Happy," and therefore your GPS on occasion gets all passive aggressive on you, it can do so by trying to steer you in the wrong direction just to see if you're paying attention. If you type in "Snæfell," and you're out east, for example, and you're not quite sure where the Snæfell you want is located, you might unwittingly pick the wrong one, and then, as we like to say, you're screwed. There's a Flatey Island out here, and there's a Flatey Island up near Húsavík. For that matter, there's Húsavík, and then there's Húsaavík, out on the east coast. Or if you're out here on the Snæfellsnes peninsula, and you want to go to Þingvellir, you might end up still on Snæfellsnes, a few kilometers from Stykkishólmur, because there's another Þingvellir there. Another Þingvellir! And yes, I realize there are many places in the world with the same name. I just am not aware of those places being so close to each other as they are here in Iceland, and if the place names are as unfamiliar to you as they were to me when I started my Iceland research, it's really easy to mistake one name for another. So when you set your GPS, just make sure you're going where you think you're going!

(By the way, I'm not sure if saying Snæfellsnes peninsula is like saying "ATM machine" — that is, redundant. I've been trying to figure these things out as I go, like yesterday, when I referred to Vatnsdalsfjall instead of Vatnsdalsfjall Mountain, the way I first typed it. I looked it up and determined that would essentially be like saying Vatnsdals Mountain Mountain. I think. Anyway, my point is, I'm not sure if I'm supposed to call it "Snæfellsnes" or "the Snæfellsnes peninsula." I sort of think it's just Snæfellsnes, but I'll keep adding "peninsula" to help clarify that I'm talking about the peninsula, since I know from experience that for easily confused people like me, all these unfamiliar Icelandic place names can be confusing until you've been staring at them for months.)

At any rate, regardless of whether Snæfellsjökull actually leads you to the center of the Earth, many people say it has one of the seven most powerful fields of mystical energy on Earth, or something like that. Maybe today I'll have my epiphany! I eat a quick breakfast at the hotel, try to get gas at the convenient gas station next door — which, it turns out, doesn't open until 10 a.m. — and then I'm on my way, on the alert for Wisdom as it undoubtedly flies through the Snæfellsnes air and into my brain via energy fields. Or however that works. I'm ready.

So I'm driving along, my favorite morning hours, and this looks to be one of the best, sunniest days I have had yet. I am heading around the western curve of the peninsula, and I see a sign pointing to Öndverðarnes. I pass by it on my way to my first stop, Hellnar, but the name sticks in my head. Öndverðarnes, Öndverðarnes, Öndverðarnes …

It's not until I'm almost at Hellnar that I make the connection.

Do you remember my first day here, just after my luxurious massage at Blue Lagoon? I was new to my car, new to my GPS, new to Iceland, and I was trying to find a place named Öndverðarnes, a place with a lighthouse. And my GPS couldn't find it. And later I decided maybe it's because I was typing in "Ond…" instead of "Önd…"? Remember that?

Remember my conversation, above, minutes ago, about places having the same name?

So, as it turns out, there's an Öndverðarnes, an inland farm in south Iceland, without a lighthouse. This is the Öndverðarnes I found on the map when I was planning my visit, and therefore I put it on my itinerary on the day I was going to be in that area in the south, my first day here. And there's an Öndverðarnes out here, at the westernmost point of the peninsula. And it has … wait for it … a lighthouse.

Coincidentally enough, I saw the lighthouse from the road as I was driving, and stopped to zoom in and take a picture of it. I had no idea that this was the very same lighthouse I'd been expecting to find on the first day, but nonetheless, I saw it. I guess I can check that one off the list, after all.

Hellnar! As I set my GPS for Hellnar on Snæfellsnes's southern shore, I think to myself, "Pam, you really need to remember to write on your itinerary WHY you want to visit a place, not just that you want to visit it. What the heck is in Hellnar? Why is Hellnar so important?" And thus I approach Hellnar knowing not what awaits me. A giant statue? A fabulous museum? A waterfall? A hike? A lighthouse? An elf?

No, gentle reader, it was none of these, but luckily enough Hellnar is small enough that when I see it, I know why I am here. In Hellnar, it is this beach. I walk the tight, mildly steep, grassy, flowered path down to the beach and find myself surrounded by a spectacular assortment of rocks of all shapes. The beach is split in two by a long concrete boat ramp. A white rowboat with turquoise trim is tied up on the beach to the right of the ramp. Out of long-time habit, I scan the beach for wishing rocks; I haven't seen any in Iceland yet, and don't know if there are any here. The left part of the beach, though, the eastern part, is where the true beauty is. For once, I don't see the omnipresent, ubiquitous hexagonal basalt pillars; instead, the walls of the interior cliff and the protruding cliff called Valasnös are covered in waves of stone. I don't know what kind of rock it is, but the word "shale" pops into my head, as the layers of stone are reminiscent of flakes on a grand scale. Whatever this pale rock is, the ocean and time have carved curves and crests and sweeps and swells of stone into the cliffside.

In contrast to the rough, angular shapes of the cliffs, the beach is strewn with oval stones. Some are smooth and flat; others are lava rocks, pitted with thousands of holes. In other places, solid, smooth chunks of rock undulate in waves under the loose pebbles. From near white to a charcoal black, the rocks are every shade of gray. Land formation eye candy. A bright cave or cove or arch is tucked between Valasnös and the main part of the land; light streams onto the aquamarine water of the cove from the ocean side, so there must be more than one opening to the cave. I move closer, and a break in the ceiling of the cave reveals itself. This is hidden cove perfection. I can imagine a girl detective coming here with her sidekicks for a picnic, and along the way being caught up in adventure and mystery and hidden watery treasure.

A couple from France is sharing the beach with me and another young couple, sitting on rocks and soaking in the bright sun. When I first got here, I talked briefly in the parking lot with the French husband about where we'd been so far and where we were going. (The wife was there, but didn't say anything, so either she doesn't speak much English or chose not to. The husband's English was far from fluent, but on the other hand, my French is nonexistent.) Now, the husband comes up to me holding two rocks, a look of joy on his face. In broken English, he explains to me that this rock is named for the fact that it makes a melodic sound when it is hit. He strikes one stone against the other to demonstrate. I can't quite understand what he's telling me, but I'm delighted that he's so excited about these melodic rocks that he wanted to share this discovery with me.

Back up at the parking lot, there are signs for a two-and-a-half kilometer walking path from Hellnar to Arnarstapi, which is my next stop. I'm sure it's quite a lovely walk, but today I'm driving. On my way out of the village, I stop to photograph the town's church, traditional white with red roof, set against the backdrop of a perfect blue sky and the wide gray volcano, slathered with a layer of bright white snow and ice at its peak. A more picturesque setting you'd be hard-pressed to find.

Leaving town, I am intrigued by a set of cabins, olive green with gray roofs and crisp white window panes. Are these homes? Rentals? Could a person stay there? They sit, clustered together, nothing between them and the glacier but a vast expanse of land waiting to be explored. It is tempting. This could be another place I'd bring friends and family for a week or long weekend. We'd wake up early in the extended sunrise; we'd go out on hikes to Arnarstapi or down to my favorite hidden cove at Hellnar or to Djúpalónssandur, which I have been trying to find, as yet unsuccessfully; we'd wander Snæfellsjökull waiting for the mystical energy to infuse us with Wisdom; we'd find secret waterfalls and go spelunking in lava caves. We'd hike out to Öndverðarnes and explore the lighthouse and read the sagas to each other; we'd watch for seals at Ytri Tunga Beach. One day we'd take a ferry on a day trip out to see the countless islands of Breiðafjordur, or even an overnight trip to the Westfjords where we'd explore Rauðisandur (Redsand) beach; another day we'd head out to one of the various horse farms and ride into the long sunset, or as long as our saddle-sensitive behinds could last. Then at night we'd sit inside playing games and chatting and laughing and drinking cocoa and Björk liqueur or Birkir snaps, the Icelandic liquors made from birch trees. This is that kind of setting. As I drive by, I see a man get out of his car and head to the door of one of the cottages, and I am a bit envious. I make a note to try to learn more about them when I get home.

Arnarstapi is a spread-out village, with several houses and cabins situated along the road that leads to the tiny town's center, far back from the cliffs. I wonder if these, too, are rentable? This would be the perfect area for a family from Reykjavík to own a cabin, to getaway on weekends or vacations. As I drive in, I see lots of people congregating around a statue/monument up on a hill. I assume that's where I am supposed to go. My GPS, however, is insisting I go farther down the road, so I follow it to see where it might lead. It takes me to the very end of the road, where there's a little dock and some people doing fishing-related business, and a small deck overlooking the water below. I snap some pictures of the boats, the grassy-topped stacks of lava rising out of the water, and of a much-photographed house sitting in the shadow of Stapafell, a pyramid-shaped volcanic mountain that is said to be home to more hidden people. It seems this peninsula is a haven for the hidden people, probably because of the mystical magic and the solitude. I haven't seen any yet, but they are, after all, hidden. I don't blame them for choosing to live in this stunning place.

On my way out, I intend to go back and investigate what the people were looking at over by the big stone monument, but I get distracted trying to decide whether to stop and take a picture of a restaurant/bar that is built to look like an old turf house. I mean, I guess it technically is a turf house. But if it was constructed in modern age to resemble a turf house, in order to draw tourists and attention, then is that genuine and should I take a picture? And does it matter? And it's only 10:30; am I really even hungry yet? I don't want to go in and order something just to order something. I'm really thirsty, but do I want to stop here when I'll probably stop somewhere else soon?

And thus I pass the monument and forget to stop and see what there was to see.

Onward to Búðir, a little hamlet with a hotel and old church, and, what I'm heading there for, supposedly a golden-sand beach. As I arrive at the dark-charcoal-gray church, two large green tour buses have just parked and unloaded their travelers. One tour guide is leading them down toward the cemetery, so I head in the opposite direction instead and briefly admire the church. My goal is the beach, though, so I head down to the hotel to see if I can find it from there. From the hotel, I can see the sand. I roam the area, trying to find a trail to the beach.

There's no obvious path, at least, not that I see. Eventually, I follow a couple of faint tire trails in the grass, to see where they might lead. A tiny parting of the grass, barely a path, heads off the tire trail to the left. I pick my way through the grass for about thirty feet, and am rewarded as the trail opens up to a tiny pocket of golden-sand beach. I don't know my beach terminology; this might be a sandbar rather than a beach; something about it feels more sandbar-like, even if I don't quite know what that is. If I were up for a dip, I could swim across some shallow water to a larger sandbar, but I'm content with my own secluded pocket beach.

It's lunchtime now. I decide to take Highway 54 across the peninsula back to the north side, grab some food at the grocery store in Ólafsvík, have a rest, and then see where the day takes me. Djúpalónssandur is actually next on my itinerary, but no matter what spelling I use, I cannot get my GPS to agree with me that it exists. I've decided it's on my way, so I'll just keep my eyes open.

Highway 54, as it cuts across Snæfellsnes, is paved. That is, it is paved until it is not. The part where it is not is when I'm on the steep downhill side, and my car feels incredibly out of my control. I slow down to a near crawl. Anytime I start to get comfortable and speed up a bit, I see a curve, and as I brake to slow down for the curve I can feel my car slipping precariously on the loose rocks. This is not a good feeling. I know I will fly off the road if I have to brake suddenly for anything, so I simply grit my teeth once more and drive as slowly as I can. As usual, there aren't too many other cars around, so at least I'm not holding anyone back.

On the way back into Ólafsvík I realize there's an overlook from which one can look out over the beach and the town. I pull in to look out at the black sand expanse below, and I wonder why

I never see anyone walking along the beaches. Is it merely because the areas are isolated? Is there no way to actually get down to the beach? What keeps the people of Iceland from enjoying their beaches? Another woman has also stopped at the overlook. Her camera is easily three times as big as mine. I'd thought my camera was huge, but here in Iceland, compared to those of so many other travelers, it is miniscule.

Without an answer to my beach ponderings, I get gas at the N1 station and then find my way to the grocery store I'd seen on the way in yesterday. I don't need gas yet but too many times I have encountered stations that were not open when I needed them. Now, I should be set all the way back to Reykjavík tomorrow, at which point I'll fill up one last time as per my rental agreement, and then return the car for good.

Now. The grocery store. Let's talk about food.

As I've indicated before, if you rely on restaurants here you'll quickly find your pocketbook empty. Even in a grocery store the food isn't cheap, but it's still just a fraction of what you'd pay at a restaurant. However, I'm noticing that grocery stores in small towns don't have much prepared food; that is, food that doesn't have to be heated up or in some other way prepared in a kitchen before you can eat it. I find this to be the case here in Ólafsvík as well, so I spend a good while looking at the few foods, other than junk food, that I can eat without cooking. You'll remember that Icelandic has enough similarities to German that I could tell kartö-flusalat is potato salad, but what is this hrásalat? I have figured out that skinka is ham (not skunk, thank goodness). But what is hrá? It's too close to hákarl for me to trust it, even despite the fact that I can't imagine grocery stores sell much fermented shark (I haven't seen it once, though admittedly I haven't looked closely), and certainly not fermented shark salad. Seriously.

I need not fear. Hrá is not shark of any kind. Hrásalat is, apparently, a sort of coleslaw. A clerk at the store helps me out, translating the ingredients list. She says it has carrots and pineapple in it, so it may be a slightly different coleslaw than what I'm used to, but it is perfectly harmless. I'm not sure about carrots and pineapple together, though, so I go with potato salad again.

I know. Some people think that experiencing odd foods is just a part of travel. Some people will judge me for not throwing caution to the wind and trying something new. Those people perhaps don't remember the time I tried something new when I was in Australia, not Australian food even, but new to me. I think it was an Ethiopian restaurant? Maybe? And I had something wrapped in grape leaves. And I spent much of the next day intimately getting to know the inside of an Australian bathroom. No, give me familiar foods and a calm stomach. Judge me all you like. You can have your fermented shark and your night spent running to the toilet. I will take my familiar foods and my time spent on adventures rather than in bed or praying to the porcelain gods, thank you very much.

After lunch back at the hotel, I'm ready to head out again. Quaint little Grundarfjörður has stuck in my mind since I passed by it yesterday on my way in, so I decide to grab my laptop and head over, to see if I can find a café somewhere and catch up on writing this book before all the memories fade into nothingness. I fill my bag full of all the usual stuff: camera, notebook, iPhone, local phone, wallet, a few thises, and a few thats. I add a bottle of water, my coat, and my laptop. I set it down and drive off.

This is one of the rare times on my trip where I'm driving a road more than once, and this time I'm heading in the other direction, east rather than the west I drove it originally. I see waterfalls and caves I hadn't seen yesterday, and I think about the fact that what you see largely depends on where you're coming from.

I ponder the literal and metaphorical implications of this idea. A few days ago I described Iceland as a combination of Switzerland and Ireland. But maybe it's much more like Norway, or Alaska, or some other place I've never been. What I see depends on where I'm coming from. And of course it's the same with people, with relationships.

But there's a waterfall, and I must get a picture! So my insightful reverie is disrupted. I stop, take a picture, continue on. I'm almost to Grundarfjörður, ready for some tea and some writing.

Inexplicably, my car suddenly starts beeping at me. No warning lights. I wasn't speeding. I check to see if the doors are all closed; they are. My seatbelt is on. What the heck? The beeps are intermittent, sporadic. I look again; still no lights at all. Nothing to give me a clue as to what is happening. The beeps continue. I start to worry that I'll have to drive the rest of the way back to Reykjavík tomorrow with this random, unpredictable, high-pitched beep. Does it mean my car is about to explode? Is something about to give out? I don't have a clue, and I am a bit worried.

But this, my friends, this is why I bought that phone! You remember the one, back on my second day here, when I did a little housekeeping before heading out? This is its purpose. I have, I believe, thirty minutes of air time. I drive the rest of the way to Grundarfjörður and stop outside a gas station. I find the rental car agency phone number on a piece of paper I tucked into the glove compartment, and I dial.

Nothing happens.

This phone is confusing me. I don't know why unfamiliar cell phones are so confusing to me, but they are. I push any number of buttons in all sorts of combinations. I manage to find the way to log onto Facebook, which would be great if that would help. It would not. Finally, after somehow adding the rental agency as a contact, I manage to dial.

Female voice on the other end: "[Icelandic I don't understand]?"

Me: "Um, do you speak English?"

Lovely rental car lady: "Yes, how can I help?"

Oh, good. She can speak English, that's a good start. "So, I have a car I rented from you guys, and it started beeping at me. I wasn't speeding, it wasn't the door, it wasn't the seatbelt. I've had the car for a week, and everything has been fine."

She is calm, cool, and reassuring in her lack of panic. "Is it showing you any lights?"

"No lights."

"Where are you?" she asks.

Oh sure, lady. Here I am, starting to perspire and in a state of distress, and you want me to try to tell you the name of this town? At this moment "Grundarfjörður" only registers in my mind as an enormously long word starting with G. I know Snæfellsnes, but can I pronounce it? I give it a go: "I'm on the Sn-eye-fet-tle-s-ness-ss peninsula," I say slowly, sounding out the letters in ones and twos, extending the word far beyond its normal number of syllables and hoping I'm close enough that she'll recognize what I'm trying to say.

"Snæfellsnes," she says, pronouncing it correctly. "Hold on." She puts me on hold, and I hold. Thirty minutes of air time, that's all I have. Come back soon, Rental Car Lady! Oh, good, she's back. "Okay, is this peeping, is it constant or does it start and stop?" Peeping. I said beeping, she heard peeping. She giggles as she says "peeping."

"It's random. Starts and stops."

"Do you have a bag in the passenger seat?"

Do I what? What has that got to do with anything?

"Yes?"

"It could be the weight of the bag. If the bag weighs too much it will signal the peep for the seatbelt."

Well, it's really more of a beep than a peep, but I suppose that's semantics. "Huh. Okay." I am somewhat unconvinced.

"See if that is it. If not, call me back."

"Okay. Hopefully that's it!" I am hopeful not just because I want the peeping to stop, but also because I'm not sure I could figure out how to dial her again if I tried.

"Yes, hopefully that is it," she says, clearly less concerned than I am.

"Thank you so much," I say. "Goodbye."

"Goodbye."

So I take the bag off the seat, leave the laptop, and cross my fingers.

And what do you know, that seems to solve the problem.

Let's back up, dear readers, to see how this happened.

As I neared Grundarfjörður, I noticed that waterfall I hadn't seen before, as it was easy to miss coming from the other direction. It had quite a fall — not just one big drop, but rather six or seven steps of falls. Fabulous! I must take a picture of this, must I not? Of course, there was absolutely nowhere to pull over. But I looked at the road, noted that I was well within a long stretch of road where people could see me for a long way both coming and going, and I decided to just stop in the road. It happens a lot, actually; people seem to do it all the time. The thing is just make sure that as I said, people can see your car from far away whether they're going your direction or coming at you. There's not so much traffic that people won't be able to go around you. You just need to make sure they can see you a good distance in advance.

So anyway, I stopped, and pulled out my camera from my bag, which I realized I'd put on the floor of the passenger seat rather than on the seat like I usually do. The laptop was on the seat, so I guess my subconscious just decided not to put the heavy bag on top. After taking the picture, though, my conscious mind decided I didn't want to risk my camera rolling around on the floor, so I set the bag on the seat on top of the laptop. So now I had the full weight of the bag, the water bottle, my laptop, and my coat on the passenger seat, and apparently that weighed enough that the car thought it could be a small child without a carseat. The peeping was intermittent probably because occasional bumps in the road caused the contents of the seat to shift just slightly up and down, decreasing and increasing the weight of the load on the seat. When it got heavier, it would peep.

I am quite relieved. I'm no mechanic and am useless around car troubles. I'm agitated and mentally off my game now, though, and not really in a space to write anymore. I check out a couple cafés, but am not sure they'd welcome someone sitting there taking up space for a couple hours (even if I did buy a tea and a snack), so I turn my car around and head to the hotel at a leisurely pace, stopping at spots I'd decided on the way over that I'd stop at on the way back.

The first stop is a cute little waterfall, Kirkjufellsfoss. This waterfall is a smaller one, with some power but still manageable, a personal-sized waterfall with a small pool at its base. It's off the road far enough (and quite remote out here in Snæfellsnes, too) that there are only a few other people here, two people heading back to the road from the waterfall, and a mother with two kids sitting on rocks far downstream from the falls. Standing at the pool, I think, this is the perfect little waterfall. If I lived here, especially if I were a kid, I'd be here every day in summer, splashing around under the falls. I don't think the pool is very deep, though I don't test that theory. At any rate, just as I am leaving, four local teenage boys I saw a few minutes ago at one of the cafés in Grundarfjörður pull up on their bikes. Yes! I am delighted to see people — local people — enjoying this perfect spot. I leave them to play in their waterfall, smiling to myself as I go. Halfway back to my car I turn to look, and sure enough, they have stripped down to their swim shorts, and are wading in.

On the way back to the hotel, I see my third police car. Nothing exciting. Until! I see it coming back the other way, chasing a car! And pulling it over! This is great excitement. Relatively speaking. People do speed a good bit on these roads. I suspect this is because they know there just aren't a lot of police out there. But when there are, they are apparently alert and on the watch.

For dinner, I decide to try a café I saw just a couple blocks down the road from Hotel Hellissandur, called Kaffi Sif. As I walk in, I see I'm the only one there except for two women huddled conspiratorially around a computer and grinning at whatever is on the screen. They see me and leap up; I learn one women is the owner, Sif Svavarsdóttir, and the other is her sister. I order by my usual standard: whatever is cheapest. In this case, it's a ham and cheese sandwich. As Sif and her sister prepare the meal, I check out the café. There's a piano to one side, and some playful art. Old tables and chairs and knickknacks along the shelves add character to a room that is otherwise crisp and clean. Sif appears at the counter, so I go to chat with her about the Björk and Birkir birch liquors I've seen but haven't yet tried. (You remember them — they're the liquors I and my friends will be drinking in the evenings after our busy days when we rent that fabulous cottage in Hellnar that I was daydreaming about yesterday!) She offers me a taste of the Björk, and it is far too delicious. I am now going to have to wrangle with myself for the rest of the trip over whether I actually need to buy some to take home. We chat more, and she tells me she has been running this cafe for six years. This summer has been hard for the business, as the weather has not been good and people have been taking their vacations elsewhere. She says running the café is difficult and expensive, but, "I love it. Every day I love my work." We talk about the joy of following your passion in life, how it changes everything. When I go to pay, I see Sif hasn't charged me for the Björk. "Our treat," says her sister as she rings me up. If you go to Hellissandur, give Kaffi Sif a try and tell them I said hello.

I am in bed at my usual time; I can barely stay awake until 10 every night. Just before midnight, though, I wake up. Realizing it's midnight, and therefore my chance to report back on exactly how dark it is as one day fades into the next at this time of year, at this place on the map, I look out the window. The sky is already lighting up with the sunrise (or is it still the sunset?); the blue is not light, but not dark, either. I take a few pictures, and go back to sleep.

If I go back:

I don't know why I didn't go down the road to Öndverðarnes, especially since I had plenty of time. I think it looked like a gravel road, and that stopped me, but looking at my map, it looks like the road might actually be paved. Or maybe I just didn't feel like driving more, after driving so much the day before and, for that matter, the whole week before. At any rate, down at Öndverðarnes is a lighthouse, as we've discussed, a bright orange squared-off rectangular box of a lighthouse, and apparently south of Öndverðarnes are the black cliffs of Svörtuloft, which is supposed to be a good place to watch the waves. Öndverðarnes is also significant, I believe, in the saga of Eyrbyggja.

I missed Gerðuberg because I didn't know about it. Places in Iceland can be hard to research; often the search engines can't find what you're looking for, or find the wrong thing. This Gerðuberg is not the one in Reykjavík that you might find easily; rather, this is a rather impressive escarpment of thick hexagonal columns, for once not trapped behind a waterfall or on the side of a cliff. Gerðuberg is at the armpit of Snæfellsnes peninsula, just north of Eldborg Crater. It would have been an easy detour on the way back to Reykjavík.

I tried to get to Djúpalónssandur but could never figure out where it was, and my GPS was no help. Djúpalónssandur is said to be one of the gems of the peninsula, a black sand beach with interestingly shaped clumps of lava, wreckage from a British fishing trawler, and some "lifting stones" — huge, round stones that sailors apparently used to lift to test their strength. I can't quite figure out why I had such trouble finding it. Had I paid better attention to printed maps rather than relying on GPS (again!), I could probably have found this supposedly spectacular spot. It's on the southwest coast of the peninsula; I was on Highway 574 and only had to turn off on Highway 572 to get there. Next time!

Looking again at the satellite map of Búðir, I now wonder if there's a road, turning off Highway 54 further east than I did, that I could have taken to get to the larger sandbar that I said I could swim to. It might be a private road. The people at Hotel Búðir would likely know.

Back to Reykjavík

Wednesday, August 7, 2013

I'm naked.

The power is out.

The hotel fire alarm is blaring.

But I'm not worried. I'm pretty sure there's not an actual emergency. You see, I think I caused the power outage. And the alarm.

With my hair dryer.

Every place I've stayed at so far has provided a hair dryer. (And, they've all been securely attached to the wall or drawer or some other part of the bathroom, which makes me wonder, is hair dryer theft a common problem in Iceland I've never heard about? People leave their cars unlocked with valuables inside, but hair dryers are anchored to the wall?)

I've been using the hotel hair dryers because they're convenient, but I did bring my own. Normally, I check with hotels in advance to see if they provide hair dryers, but I never got around to it this time. What's more, I forgot to ask Mary Frances whether she has a dryer I can use. So I brought my own.

In previous hotels I've stayed at on this trip, the hair dryers have been adequate. Adequate enough that I've used them. This hotel, however, has the kind of hair dryer where you have to keep your thumb on the switch to keep it turned on — and when it takes as long as it takes me to dry my hair, that's a sure recipe for a thumb cramp. I take one look at it, think, "Heck with that," and pull out my own dryer. I've lugged it all this way; I may as well use it!

I swap the power adapter from my phone, which has been charging, to the hair dryer, and plug it in. Flip the dryer to "on" and "high." For twenty seconds or so, we're good. And then …

The power goes out. I start wondering whether there might be a fuse box within the room itself, but then …

The fire alarm comes on.

So here I am, naked in the hotel room, and the power is out, and the fire alarm is going throughout the whole hotel and can probably be heard all over town, and I'm pretty sure it's all my fault.

I start to get dressed. I hadn't set out any clothes for today yet, and I am not a master packer, so I have to dig through the whole suitcase to find the various items I need. The alarm continues. I'm in my underwear, still not presentable to the outside world. The alarm goes on. I find shirt, pants, socks. My shoes that can be slipped on quickly (in the case of an emergency, such as a fire alarm, for example) are at the very bottom of my suitcase, wrapped tidily in plastic bags. The fire alarm is still going. I pull out my shoes. I'm finally dressed, and …

The fire alarm goes off.

But my power does not come back on.

So now I'm in my room, dressed, hair dripping wet, power still off.

The phone rings.

It's the front desk. "Just checking to see if everything is okay?"

Oh dear. What do they know? Do they know I caused the morning's pandemonium? Or do they just (somehow) know I never made it out of my room?

"I'm fine," I say, nonchalantly, admitting nothing. "But my power's out."

"Your power is out? Okay, I will look into that."

"Thank you."

I mean, it's not like I *tried* to make the power go out. It's not like I went down the hall and pulled the fire alarm in a drunken hysteria. It just happened, right? I had a hair dryer and a power adapter. I used them. It happens.

My original plan for the morning was to go down for breakfast, come back up, take my time packing (it's a short driving day today, just a hop back to Reykjavík), check out, and leave. But now, I start thinking about the lock to my room, and the fact that it's a key card. Electronic.

I have no idea how long the power will be out. If I leave the room, will I be able to get back in? I'm convinced the door will shut behind me and the key card won't work (I had some issues with it yesterday, after all, and had to get a new card).

So I change my plan of action. I get myself completely packed up (putting my hair back in a ponytail; I guess it will have to do for today). I check the room for stray power adapters and phones plugged into outlets and clothes hanging in the closet. Everything is accounted for (including my hair dryer). Water bottle refilled. Car keys zipped into the side pocket of my bag.

I have not packed particularly lightly for this trip. I know, I know. No one ever wishes they'd packed heavier. It's true. There are things I've not used, that could have stayed home, and things I've not used that I probably needed to have along anyway. The tripod, I didn't need. The rain jacket, I wouldn't have come without. The multiple pairs of shoes, I could argue for either way. I've gone on trips with just one pair of shoes, and let me tell you, those shoes were ripe by the end of the trip. Still, I didn't need the water-tolerant shoes that I'd brought along in case I needed them for hot pools and Blue Lagoon. Regardless, everything I brought is all here with me now. I lug it outside into the hallway, room key in hand. Am I really going to take all this down to the breakfast room with me?

The door latches behind me. The moment of truth. Will the key card work?

It works. All that early packing for nothing.

I push the suitcase and small rolling carry-on back inside the dim room, and head downstairs to breakfast. After I eat, I turn in my key and, feeling guilty that I *completely unintentionally* caused a fire alarm, and they seem to know it, I explain that I was just using my hair dryer, officer, I swear that's all I was doing. The woman at the front desk laughs and says, "That probably did it!" I am curious, but don't ask, whether everyone else in the building ran outside while I was busy slowly getting dressed. I will never know how much of a commotion I caused.

I am determined not to drive one more mile of gravel road if I don't have to, so I decide to take the road around the tip of Snæfellsnes again, rather than cutting across the peninsula to the south side. This will give me another chance at Arnarstapi, though the weather isn't nearly as glorious today as it was yesterday.

In Arnarstapi, my GPS again wants me to go to the end of the road (yes, I set the GPS, even though I know where I'm going now and could not possibly miss it), but this time I stop at the giant rock statue I drove by yesterday. At first I think it's a monument of some sort, but on closer inspection it looks like a giant squatty armless troll, made out of flat slabs of rock, complete with beard and over-hanging eyebrows and a long rust-colored nose. As it turns out, I'm right: The statue is of Bárðr Snæfellsáss, from the Bárðar saga Snæfellsáss ok Gests (that is, it's a guy from an Icelandic saga). His mom was human but his dad was half giant, half troll. At one point, Bárðr disappeared and faded into the Snæfellsjökull ice cap and became the guardian spirit of the mountain. There's more to the saga than that, obviously, including a magic candle and a wom-an who floated to Greenland, unharmed, as one does. After all, it's a saga. Those things weave and wend and have as much drama as any modern day reality show, only more complex. And perhaps more believable. Magic candles, right? I can get behind that.

I briefly wonder whether this is all I missed yesterday; whether all those people flocking here were here just to see Bárðr. (There are no people here today, probably due to the weather and the early hour.) But then, behind Bárðr, I glimpse a trail. In what I assume is an attempt to help control mud, the pathway is covered in large rubber tiles with holes in them. Clearly, this path must be well used, and there must be a reason for that! I follow the trail out to the cliff's edge; there's a section of cliff that juts out just enough that I can look back at the face of the rest of the cliffs behind me. Jackpot! This is what I wanted to see! Here again are my beloved basalt columns, dark charcoal pillars stretching from the clifftop down to the beach below. Eons of crashing waves have carved mul-tiple caves deep into the columns, including one cave just to the west of the promontory I'm on, and another just to the east. I gaze longingly at the west cave. With the tide where it is now, the cave floor is dry and inviting. I imagine climbing down (one should not do this; I'm sure it's quite dangerous), and setting up house in that cave, inviting people over for a little tea by the sea. I don't know what it is about hidden caves that entices me, but they always spark my imagination.

It's extremely windy today, though, and my air-dried hair is whipping around my face, so I cut my time short. Yesterday, I looked up Arnarstapi to see what people come here for. As amazing as these caves are, they're not the subject of most of the pictures I saw. Judging from the scenery in the pictures, I suspect the photos I saw online were taken closer to the place I stopped yesterday. I follow my GPS's wishes and drive back down to the end of the road.

There's a trail out to the west, which I walk toward until I see signs indicating it's private property. I back down. Then, I see another narrow trail — a path worn down in the grass, really — that leads up a hill, so I give that a try. Sure enough, after a few hundred feet I look down and find myself looking at the scene I've seen in all the pictures, of a sort of cove with more lava stacks standing boldly in the water. I can imagine that in yesterday's dazzling sunshine this view would have been particularly spectacular, but even today it still holds its charm. The rock formations in this area are magnificent.

Back in the car, I pass by more sights I visited yesterday. After Búðir, I am back in unexplored (to me) country. And sure enough, the road on this southern route of the peninsula is paved the whole way. The tour buses must drive out from Reykjavík along the southern rather than the northern road, which makes sense. I don't know if the tour buses travel the paved roads, or the roads are paved where the tour buses want to go, but the closer you get in to Reykjavík, the more paved roads there are.

I find myself greatly amused when I drive by a sign that points to "Borg" and "Minni-Borg"; I have to stop myself from turning around to take pictures. Star Trek fans will understand.

I've planned a stop at a museum today, which is quite unusual for me. I generally enjoy museums, but only for a short amount of time. I would rather experience a thing, I suppose, than be in a museum that explains the things. And there's something creepy to me about folk museums, where they take mannequins and dress them up appropriate to the era in question, and pose them in tasks they'd be doing back in their day. It's possible I have a slight fear of mannequins. Not fear. They're just creepy. And then when they're in a museum, and they don't get dusted, but their lifeless unblinking dusty eyes still follow you around the room, that's creepy.

The museum I'm going to today is The Settlement Centre, located in the town of Borgarnes, which has a surprising lack of accented vowels and should not be confused with the northwest town of Blönduós, although in my mind I do, over and over. Hopefully, I will not run into any creepy mannequins in either the exhibits or the town.

Borgarnes feels huge. Driving in, I feel vulnerable and confused by all the cars and traffic and roads. I instantly miss the peace and calm I've grown used to over the last week. The people and traffic feel like chaos, but my GPS guides me through it all gently until I reach The Settlement Centre unharmed.

The parking lot is completely full, both cars and buses, not one spot left. I remember Mary Frances telling me that in Reykjavík, "If someone's not already parked there, it's a parking spot." Is that true in Borgarnes, as well? Can I just find an empty area, and park? I look around and it seems some people think the answer is, "Yes," but I manage to find a reasonably legitimate parking spot a half a block away from the Centre.

The Centre has two main exhibits, along with a sizeable gift shop and café. I decide to go through both exhibits, which are toured with the aid of audio guides, offered in multiple languages. An elderly man gives me the audio guide for the first exhibit, checks to make sure it's set to "English," tells me that the guide will tell me I can't take pictures, but that the guide is wrong and I may in fact do so, then sends me on my way into the exhibit.

The first exhibit talks about the settlement of Iceland, complete with a moving replica of a ship's bow to simulate the rough waters the first settlers would have faced on their trip over, and some strange pods along the walls that are supposed to be representations of early Icelandic leaders. But instead, they look far more like props from an alien movie in which people have been cryogenically frozen into the walls, and then their bodies disintegrated so all that's left is the frozen somewhat body-shaped outline where the body once was. I am not sure that's the look they were going for, but if it was, they nailed it.

The second exhibit takes visitors through the tale of Egil's saga, which tells the story of Egil Skallagrímsson, an Icelandic farmer, Viking, and poet. This exhibit features scenes from the saga depicted in wonderful artistic variety by a number of artists, as well as a rather frightening, full-height statue of a man wearing a wolf hat, and a gruesome horse's head on a stick. Apparently if you got really mad at someone you might jab a horse head on a stick, and throw curses in the general direction of the person you were mad at. It was called a "scorn pole," and from the state of the horse's head on the pole, apparently it works best if the horse's head is partially decomposed. No creepy mannequins, after all, but I wasn't counting on a horse head! I'm hoping it doesn't give me nightmares.

I get gas at Borgarnes and stop at another grocery store for a quick meal, and then am back on the road.

Shortly after Borgarnes, there is a tunnel. I knew about this tunnel, but had completely forgotten about it and had forgotten to plan for it before heading out today. Why would I need to plan for it? Because it's a toll tunnel. This is an underwater tunnel, under Hvalfjörður, thus Hvalfjarðargöng. I've also seen it written as Hvalfjarðargöngin, and I wonder if that hearkens back to what Car Rental Guy told me about "inn" at the end of things, thus making it THE Hvalfjörður tunnel? Except that it's just "in," not "inn," which mostly means that once again I am confused. The Icelandic language has bested me yet again.

At any rate, there's a tunnel, and it goes under water, and to drive it you need to pay 1000 ISK each way. Lucky for me, I have some cash left. I pass a 1000 ISK bill through the little toll window and am on my way.

Hvalfjarðargöng is long, a little more than five and a half kilometers, a little under three and a half miles, and that's a little more than five and a half kilometers of a dank tube smelling like exhaust fumes. There are tons of fans in the tunnel, I assume there to try to blow the fumes out. I can't help but wonder how successful they are, or how much worse the tunnel would be without it. Numbers on the side of the tunnel tell me how far I've traveled and how far I have left to go. It is a very long five and a half kilometers, actually, and I'm out of practice of being in traffic, around other cars. Suddenly I'm aware again that I'm driving more slowly than your average car, and this is definitely a no-passing zone.

A few miles later, I emerge. The tunnel cuts what was once nearly an hour-long trip down to about seven minutes, and I'm almost to Reykjavík. Interestingly, the closer in to Reykjavík I get again, the more road warning signs I see. Out in south and east Iceland, when I was about to drive through a wind tunnel or tornado or off a cliff, there was nary a sign at all. "Abandon all hope, ye who enter here," the roads of outback Iceland might suggest. But now, I see a sign that indicates there's a section of the road coming up where cars are not allowed to pass, and I literally laugh out loud. I have driven around the country, little warning sign; I have driven over treacherous one-lane bridges and a hundred kilometers of gravel road; I have driven the washboard that is the 864 and the deathtrap that is the 939 with its twelve percent grade; I have sidled up next to cliffs and dared the wind to blow me off course. I have even, you may remember, driven on the ocean floor. The ocean floor, people! (Well, it was the ocean floor a long time ago.) No passing allowed? Warning sign, you cannot scare me.

And then, I'm driving back in the outskirts of Reykjavík, my round-the-island journey nearly complete. I'll be here for a few days, but the car will be picked up tonight. (A fabulous thing about Route 1: I picked up the car at the airport, but to return it all I had to do was give them the address where I'll be staying in Reykjavík — where the car will be parked at the appointed pick-up time — and they'll come pick it up! Could that be any more convenient?!) (No, it could not.)

I am back in the land of roundabouts, in a city with a thousand times as many people as most of the places I've been for the past eight days. I've driven more than a thousand miles around this tiny country at the top of the world. I've only done it in summer, of course; I've only witnessed Iceland in her mildest of moods and can't claim to know the country well. I can't believe this journey is almost over, that I'll be returning this dirty gas-guzzling little car that nonetheless managed to keep me safe through all I (and the country) threw at it. As I complete this odd-shaped loop around the island, I can't help but feel the country is in me now.

I top off the gas tank one last time, then my GPS guides me back to Mary Frances's parking lot. I'm early; she won't be home from work yet. I pull the bags out of the trunk and set them on the stoop, then set at going through seats and glove compartments and any possible place some belongings could hide. I pop the gas tank cover and tuck the keys inside, leaving the car unlocked as I'd been instructed by Car Rental Guy; now all that's left is for someone from Route 1 to come and take the car home.

I marvel at the idea of just leaving the car keys under the gas cover of an unlocked car. Reykjavík is like that, though; it feels safe. "You won't need theft insurance," Car Rental Guy had told me, and he's right. There were many times along my route when I left my car with all my valuables in plain sight on the passenger seat while I chased after a picture of a waterfall. At Hellnar, when I was down at the beach, eyes closed, soaking in the sun on the warm rocks, I realized I wasn't sure I'd locked the car. This was followed by the realization that in all likelihood, everything would be fine.

After a delicious lamb dinner with Mary Frances, her family, and some friends, the ladies in the group head out for a night on the town. Reykjavík is known for its nightlife, but this is Wednesday; will the city be hopping? It's already getting late when we head out, but it's still light enough to see as we make our way through Hólavallagarður, a cemetery that serves as a shortcut to our destination. We make our way first to a bar that serves beer and wine. It is, indeed, overflowing with people; the chatter fills the room and the air from floor to ceiling. When we get up to move on to another bar, our seats are filled barely moments after we leave them. It's after ten, not yet eleven. The second bar we go to is much more spacious, and while most of the tables are full, it feels like the evening party is waning fast. After another drink, we head on home.

More to do:

If you're not waterfalled-out by this point, Hraunfossar in the Húsafell/Borgarfjörður area, and nearby Barnafoss, look like winners. If I'm reading the map right, to get there I would have diverted a bit east on my way to (or after) Borgarnes. Hraunfossar looks like it's more an area of a lot of little waterfalls — maybe that's what the "ar" in "Hraunfossar" means? The entire region looks like it's worth checking out.

An English version of Egil's saga is available online at http://sagadb.org/egils_saga.en.

Days away from going to print with this book, I was pondering the fire alarm (that I may or may not have caused; there's no proof) at Hellissandur. I suddenly remembered that when I was in Scotland, within the course of two weeks, not one but two fire alarms went off in my presence. I hadn't thought about this before, but maybe it's me?! (No, there's no *Pam on the Map: Scotland (retrospective)* yet, but there could be! We went in 2009, and I'm sure I still have all those emails. We'll see!)

Reykjavík

Thursday, August 8, 2013

Naked. Again.

Power out. Again.

This morning, I saw Mary Frances and her family off, then took my shower, looking forward to having hair-dryer-dried hair today rather than waiting through the extended wet-headedness of air-drying. I plugged in my hair dryer with a tiny bit of trepidation, but with hopefulness; certainly I was hopeful. I again flipped the hair dryer switches to "on" and "high," and all was well. Ten seconds, fifteen. And then ...

So here I am, naked again. Power out again. I have broken Mary Frances's house.

I look across the hall at the bathroom (I'm drying my hair in the bedroom as the bathroom doesn't have an electrical plug). The light is on in that room. At least I didn't break the whole house.

Find the fuse box, I think to myself. I know I saw it earlier. I can fix this, I think, with somewhat less certainty.

Next to the front door, I find the fuse box. I look inside. Isn't one of the fuses supposed to have flipped itself off? Isn't that how it works? All the fuse switches are up. Since some lights are on, the fuses should not all be the same. Not all up or all down.

I send Mary Frances a meek message explaining what has happened. "Do you know which switch is the bedroom?"

I try to decipher the Icelandic, written in pencil and faded and smudged over the years. I send her the options: "Eldavil/bokoraofn; bvotlavd; ljir slodtnun/dogstops; ljir dogstops/beck og linshorb; ljir soefrakherf/gerag? Can't read the writing too well, plus: Icelandic."

She does not reply. She's at work, after all. Can't spend all day checking messages.

I don't want to leave the house broken when I go out. I feel awful. I stare at the switches.

Maybe I'll just try all of them, I think.

Nothing works.

Maybe I'll hit the yellow button.

It turns everything off. That was not my goal. I switch all the switches off, then on, and everything is as it was.

Including my bedroom, which remains off.

Hm.

And then, I realize that as I was flipping switches, the metal plate in front of them was a bit loose. Maybe I can see something else if I move the plate? Yes, it moves. I edge it out of its seat, and …

There it is. One switch, in the down position. The rogue switch, hiding behind the metal plate like a sneaky little Icelandic hidden person, making trouble.

I flip the switch. The lights come back on.

I am a Viking Fuse Ninja.

My hair dryer is a waste of luggage space. I resent having lugged it around, but what can you do? With the way the Icelandic wind whips my hair around, it's all something of a moot point anyway. Long-haired ladies (and gentlemen), you'll want to bring a hairband or two.

The delay is not for naught. I check my email and there's a message from the mayor of Akureyri. He will be in Reykjavík today and tomorrow, and might we reschedule his interview? A few emails back and forth and we've settled on a time and place. That makes three interviews (four people) tomorrow; in addition to the mayor of Akureyri, I have already scheduled interviews with two authors and the mayor of Reykjavík. I love interviewing people. I love hearing their stories and their passions. Tomorrow will be a good day.

And with that, I head out into misty Reykjavík. At the last minute I bring my travel umbrella. It is a tiny little thing, hardly qualifying as an umbrella. It unfolds to barely more than two feet wide, and when it is asked to re-fold into the compact form requested of it for storage, it often crankily refuses. An arm here or there will not fold back in on its own. Gentle nudging generally does the trick, but sturdy, this umbrella is not. However, the forecast is for rain. I don't know what Reykjavík rain is like, but I'll go out prepared.

On my way out I notice my rental car is still here. On the one hand, I'm relieved no one stole it. After all, it's unlocked and the keys are by the gas cap! On the other hand, I am hoping they won't charge me for another day. And what if it's damaged in the time between when they were supposed to pick it up last night, and when they actually pick it up? Who is responsible?

With those thoughts in mind, I head out. I've mapped out the walking route online. I take off with a printed map, and with certainty I can get there easily.

Which is ridiculous. I have an innate ability to get turned around. I walk past a tall cathedral, note on the map that I am on the right route. Landakotskirkja: Check! I continue along Túngata street. Check! And now I should be on … well … wait, that's Vonarstræti there? But What happened to Kirkjustræti? Where is that little jog in the road I was looking for? I wander down to the lake and spend five minutes staring at the map and the lake, trying to figure out why I can't figure out where I am. People wander by with maps, luggage. There are more cameras here, more American accents. The drips from the sky increase in size and speed. Then it starts to really rain. I tuck my camera away and pull out my umbrella. I stand some more, looking at my map.

Finally I figure out that I am already on the street I want to be on at this point, Lækjargata. I must have missed the street sign. I wander back north, as I have unintentionally drifted south, away from my goal. I find Bankastræti, which turns diagonally off into Skólavörðustígur, just as it's supposed to, with the iconic Hallgrímskirkja (church of Hallgrímur) capping it off at one end. Though my car and its GPS with its soothing voice are no longer with me, I hear it in my head: "Arriving at destination on left." My map is soaked and I'm not far behind, but I am where I'm meant to be.

I'm scheduled to meet a gentleman from the Reykjavík Chamber of Commerce, Ragnar Þorvarðarson, at 1:30 in front of the old prison (Hegningarhúsið or "the penalty house"), for a "traditional Icelandic ice cream car ride." Before leaving the apartment for the morning, I did an image search on the prison so I'd know what I was looking for. The dark gray facade with irregular stones and arched windows is easy to recognize, and I see it at once, about halfway down the street. Hegningarhúsið is, incidentally, the oldest prison in Iceland, though it's only about one hundred and thirty-five years old. I am surprised, regularly, that things in Iceland aren't older than they are. The country seems timeless but its human history is relatively young. Hegningarhúsið is still in use, but not heavily; it's more of a transfer point than a prison. As if to prove that it's still official, a guard comes out the door carrying a big black plastic bag. Body parts? No, probably just garbage.

But our meeting is not until 1:30, and I'm early. When Ragnar emailed me to set the date and time, he wrote "13.30." Afraid of missing our appointment, I calculated and recalculated in my head to make sure that 13.30 was indeed 1:30. As it's only noon and I haven't eaten yet, I find a café that specializes in crepes. I note that the woman who took my order spoke English from the start. I don't think it's that I looked particularly English-speaking (though I probably do). I suspect, rather, that in Reykjavík she's used to dealing with people from all over the world, so she starts with English, which is almost universally understood here. People from Spain, France, the U.S., Switzerland, Germany, everyone speaks English here.

Having time left over after a crepe (in a crowded muggy room, everyone escaping the weather), I wander the soggy streets as the skies switch back and forth between rain and downpour. Part of Skólavörðustígur is restricted to pedestrian traffic — no cars — a feature I love in a city. To escape the rain, I find a bookstore and look around for books by the authors I'll be interviewing tomorrow. I find them — in Icelandic. Seeing that the bookstore has WiFi, I pull out my iPhone and email the authors to ask if their books are available in English. One answers that hers is; the other answers that his is not. I ask a clerk at the desk for the English versions from the first author. He enthusiastically points me to her books. Clearly, he is a fan. I'm excited. The clerk is charming and helpful, as is another clerk at the counter who gives me a bit of history on the author. It suddenly occurs to me I should have done more research. Then I realize even if I had, most of what I would have found might have been in Icelandic. Still, it's on my to-do list for tonight.

I peruse a few more shops on the street. There's so much cute stuff in these stores, but I have already wildly overspent on this trip. I've finally calculated the price of gas from krona per liter into U.S. dollars per gallon, and it's just over $8 per gallon. Ouch.

About five minutes early, I head to the prison. From the other side of the street, I have my eye on a prison doorway where I plan to seek shelter from the rain while I wait. But as I cross the street, a woman on her cell phone finds the same cove. She ducks in, and then I hear that she must have pushed a buzzer. She walks by me down to the door where I saw the guard earlier, with the bag of garbage (body parts). He re-emerges from the door and lets the woman in.

So the prison is in use, after all.

Just about then, a man pulls up in a car and edges the tires slightly onto the sidewalk. I look and recognize Ragnar from his picture. I get in the car and instantly am delighted by his warm kindness. Who was it that told me Icelanders are cold? Because I have found almost every one to be so kind. Of course there are a few who are not as friendly, but that's true anywhere. Icelanders are welcoming and open, and I love them.

I found Ragnar and this ice cream car ride online, through an "Invitation to Iceland" campaign the Iceland tourism people ran in 2011. I wrote Ragnar and asked if he'd be willing to recreate his invitation for me and my book, and he said yes. I've been wondering ever since just what a "traditional Icelandic ice cream car ride" is. Do we ride around in an ice cream truck? Do we pass out ice cream to children? Do we drive to dairy farms and get milk from cows? I have no idea, and I tell Ragnar I'm excited to find out. As it turns out, I'm not sure how much of an actual tradition it is; I suspect he and his friends may have made this up. He tells me that when the weather is bad, people go out for ice cream and then drive around enjoying the treats and each other's company. Perhaps it's not from the Viking times, but I'll take it. And regardless, Icelanders do seem to have an obsession with ice cream, so it's legitimate enough for me.

We go get ice cream, and then for the next hour and a half Ragnar drives me around as we chat on all possible topics: school, the economic crash, the arts, politics, bike lanes, tourism, the Gay Pride festival which is already underway and ongoing through this weekend, the suburbs, travel, whaling, Icelanders, the Internet and social media, narrow roads, taxes, values, attitudes, priorities, and more. He identifies occasional landmarks as we pass them, but mostly we are absorbed in fascinating, engaging conversation and I barely notice where we are.

Ragnar points at a man running, and comments that people brought running back from Europe. People in Iceland didn't run for exercise not too long ago, he tells me, but now it's common. I mention a comedy sketch by a Scottish comedian named Danny Bhoy, in which Danny says Scottish people don't understand running either: Why run if no one is chasing you? Ragnar laughs and says yes, that's how it used to be here. He comments that after the economic crash, "People are knitting again," which is the second time I've heard someone comment on knitting in relation to the economic crash. I take it to mean people are returning to simpler but productive activities, things that bring friends and communities together, and that's not necessarily a bad thing. This is not to say that the crash was a good thing by any means; but some people I've talked to do seem to think it helped people reevaluate their priorities, to a positive result.

I ask Ragnar whether he thinks the advent of social media has been instrumental in bringing Iceland into the global community; he agrees that it has. Before social media, Iceland was more isolated socially, and Icelanders had fewer opportunities to interact with people around the world. Now, connecting with anyone from anywhere is as easy as getting online. Case in point: me going on an ice cream car ride with someone from the Reykjavík Chamber of Commerce.

I mention that I'm interviewing Jón Gnarr tomorrow (mayor of Reykjavík), and Ragnar tells me he had a chance to work with Jón once, and he's a great guy. The past six mayors of Reykjavík didn't make it to two years in office, but Jón is three years into a four-year term, and speculation has begun over whether he'll run again. Ragnar tells me he heard someone say that in an interview this week Jón said he wouldn't run again. I ruminate on whether I'll ask him myself. I suspect if he hasn't told his countrymen, he won't tell me, but you never know!

We talk a bit about tourism, as well. Iceland is talking a lot about tourism, Ragnar tells me, and is considering tourism from the perspective of three kinds of travelers: the bikers/hikers/backpackers, the average tourist, and the luxury tourist. I mention what I've noticed about the lack of infrastructure in the country, and he agrees it's a big challenge. About one million people visit Iceland each year, he says; that's about three times the population of the country. What kind of experience is Iceland giving them? Whom do they want to target? Right now, he says, Iceland is really only serving the biker/hiker/backpacker population well. While I've loved my trip, I have to agree. There are many places I'd be interested in seeing, but I'd have to be a biker or hiker to get to them. But, we also agree there's a dilemma in figuring out how not to destroy or compromise the Iceland that people come for, by making it more accessible. It's definitely a challenge. We chat briefly about the U.S. system of buying passes to state and national parks, which helps fund the maintenance of the lands. I gather that Iceland is open to ideas and possibilities.

As we drive by a beach, I remember noticing out at Snæfellsnes that I never see anyone on the beaches here. Why is that? I ask.

"Our beaches are too cold," he says, and instantly I realize that makes sense. Dipping one's toes into an arctic ocean isn't really the stuff of tropical dreams. There is, he tells me, a beach in Reykjavík where they pump geothermally heated water into the ocean. Nauthólsvík Geothermal Beach. The water is warm for several meters out from the shore, but then the icy ocean reclaims its chilly rights to these waters and it's cold again. Do people go there? I ask. Yes, he tells me. People love it.

Ragnar reveals to me what he says is the quintessential Icelandic phrase or philosophy: "Þetta reddast," or, basically, "Everything will work itself out." Through all their challenges, through the economic crash, through the chilly weather and long winters and everything else, Ragnar says, Icelanders always remind each other that everything will work out. He says this attitude can cause difficulties when Iceland is working with other nations that don't have the same philosophy, but Þetta reddast works well for the people of Iceland. He also tells me that Iceland's "national pastime" is calculating everything per capita. Sure, Iceland may be small; sure some countries may dismiss Iceland as insignificant. But if you calculate everything per capita, Iceland comes out shining! In a country of 320,000, every person counts.

At the end of our time, Ragnar drops me off at Mary Frances's apartment. (My rental car is finally gone.) He gives me a hug and leaves. A most pleasant way to spend a drizzly afternoon. We must have driven almost every road in town, past the Harpa concert hall and the iconic church; through the suburbs and by the malls; out to one of Ragnar's favorite places, the Grotta lighthouse; and more. And yet, having been absorbed in conversation, I saw hardly any of it. I'm not disappointed. This is the Reykjavík I'm far more interested in: the minds and souls and hearts and ideas of the people who live here; their stories, and the stories of their home.

For the rest of the afternoon, I write, catch up with friends online, and do my research for tomorrow. When Mary Frances gets home, we chat about what Ragnar told me about the country and the Icelandic people. I love traveling around a country, but I also love the opportunities like today, where I'm able to connect with people on a real, one-on-one level. The exchange of ideas, finding where we're alike and where we're not, discovering different ways to approach the world and how we maneuver our ways through it. I love that.

And, connecting with people is an especially fabulous way to spend a rainy day such as today.

Speaking of weather, I'll give you a quick Icelandic weather primer, and a lesson for those of us used to thinking in Fahrenheit.

When I was in Australia, a million years ago, I learned this handy way of converting Celsius to Fahrenheit: "Double it and add thirty." So if the weather is 10° Celsius, you double it (10x2=20) and then add thirty (20+30=50). This means 10°C is approximately 50°F. If you do the actual conversion, that's spot on. As I understand it the "double it and add thirty" method should in general get you within 4°F of the actual temperature. Not bad! Close enough that you'll know whether to wear shorts or bring a parka.

In Reykjavík, in August, the average minimum is 8°C and the average maximum is 13°C, and if you double these and add thirty, you get 46°F minimum, 56°F maximum, which means IT IS NEVER SHORTS WEATHER. And yet, with all the hot pots and pools, you'll find yourself carrying around your swimsuit as much as or more than any other trip you'll go on. (Of course these are averages. On my trip, I don't know what the actual temperatures have been but certainly in my first few days and several other days it felt warmer, more like in the 60s.) Also, remember that even though Iceland is small, the temperatures still vary across the country. The north gets much colder, much sooner. Bring layers. Bring gloves.

For what it's worth, if you're traveling when it's very cold, "double it and add thirty" works even in the negative numbers, to an extent. For example, -5°C. Double it: -5x2=-10. Add thirty: -10+30=20. If you do the actual conversion, -5°C is about 23°F, so you're close. I think, actually, that this method works best for temperatures you'd actually encounter in day-to-day weather; the further extreme you go in either high or low temperatures, the less accurate it is. We all know that 100°C is 212°F, but if you double it and add thirty you'd get 230°F, which is starting to get a ways off.

Um, so, have I ever mentioned I like numbers?

Anyway, that's Thursday. Friday, I'll do my interviews. And then Saturday, we will do Pride.

The Interviews

Friday, August 9, 2013

Fully dressed.

Power is on.

Hair is drip drying.

A few days ago I counted, and at that time according to that count I had one more day of travel left than I had pairs of clean underwear. Today, with three days left including today, I counted three pairs of clean underwear (and also three clean pairs of socks). Either I miscounted earlier, or I wore a pair twice, or a magic laundry genie came in the night and washed one pair of underwear for me. I know I didn't wear a pair twice, and I strongly suspect a magic laundry genie didn't come (and if it did, what a stingy genie, only washing one pair of underwear and leaving all the other dirty laundry), so I must have miscounted. A delightful discovery, I must say, as now I don't have to wash out one pair of undies in the sink and hope it dries in time. I did not bring quick-dry underwear on this trip. If you've read my Wishing Rock books, and you remember the diatribe on travel underwear, that is from experience. No, it's real underwear for me all the way.

I have a full day of interviews ahead, and am having a cup of tea while I prepare.

I brought copies of my own books to give away to the people I'm interviewing, and I've lugged them all around the country. I just figured out that I drove two thousand six hundred and six kilometers on this trip, or one thousand six hundred and nineteen miles, which is a long way to carry excess luggage. Still, several copies of *Letters from Wishing Rock* and a copy or two of the second and third books have made their way to Iceland. Surely this is just the beginning. Watch out, world. Wishing Rock is coming.

In preparation for flying home, I've pulled everything out of my suitcase to get organized for my final days. In the process, I've lost my comb. It is a critical item, now that I can't dry my hair. How does that happen? How do I have something one minute — it was right next to my brush — and then it's gone? That's one of the things I like least about moving around so much as I travel: Every night, something that was carefully packed away gets lost, and it takes me ten minutes to find it. I've never been on a cruise, and frankly I'm not sure I want to, but the idea of just unpacking once and then repacking once, well, that's quite appealing.

However, I will forgive the comb issue as the sun is out, which is unexpected but delightful.

I am giddy excited for Interview Day. This is one of my favorite things. This is one of the reasons I love being a writer. Asking questions, lots and lots of questions, and getting insights into people's minds and lives, seeing how their brains work, learning where their passions lie, discovering what makes their worlds turn. Being a writer is like holding a passport to the world. It gives me access to people and places and experiences that I might not otherwise have.

My enduring personality trait is intense curiosity, and writing helps me quench that thirst for knowledge. Am I a writer because I am curious, or am I curious because I'm a writer? I suspect it's the former. Writing opens up the world and helps lead me to answers.

First on my agenda for Interview Day are Yrsa Sigurðardóttir and Ragnar Jónasson, Icelandic crime fiction authors. Yrsa, who has been referred to by many as the "Queen of Icelandic crime fiction," is one of four Icelandic crime fiction authors to have her work translated into English; one of her books, *I Remember You*, is being made into a movie. Ragnar is the author of a Northern Iceland crime series, which takes place in Siglufjörður, a historic fishing village and Iceland's most northerly town. Ragnar's Siglufjörður tales are being developed into an Icelandic TV series.

I am meeting the authors today at Nordic House in downtown Reykjavík. ("Downtown" might not be the right word. Reykjavík is compact and quite walkable, but I'm not entirely sure there's a specific core.) I walk the mile or so from Mary Frances's apartment, repeating the very simple directions in my head so I don't get lost. There are only a few turns between here and there, but I am nonetheless carrying a map as backup, certain but unconcerned that it makes me look like a tourist.

There's construction on the final road leading up to Nordic House, which puts me off the sidewalk and onto the grass. As I pick my way through animal droppings in the grass, I think about the customs form I'll have to fill out to be allowed back into the U.S.: "Have you been on any farm land?" "Well, I mean, it's Iceland, so …."

Yrsa and Ragnar arrive shortly after me, and we make our introductions.

Let's digress a moment to discuss the Icelandic naming system. Iceland has what is called a "patronymic" naming system, meaning that the names don't reflect family lineage, but rather come from the father's name. (Names are occasionally matronymic, after the mother.) The children of a man named Jón would be named Jónsson if sons, and Jónsdóttir if daughters. Therefore, brothers and sisters don't have the same last names, parents don't have the same names as their children (unless a father has the same first name as his own father), and so on. People are listed in the phone book by first name; authors are sorted at the bookstore by first name. And in interviews and articles, people are listed once by their full name, and then are referred to by first name, e.g., Yrsa and Ragnar rather than Ms. Sigurðardóttir and Mr. Jónasson. (An interesting side effect of this naming system is that people can't tell from their names whether they're related. So someone created a "dating app" for phones, which lets people find out whether they're family before they … shall we say, get more intimate. The app has the tagline "bump in the app before you bump in bed." Only in Iceland.)

Anyway, they arrive and we find a small setting of chairs on which to sit. Yrsa and Ragnar are well familiar with Nordic House; they, along with English author Quentin Bates, are deep in the process of organizing "Iceland Noir," Iceland's first festival of crime fiction, which will be held here in November this year. Arnaldur Indriðason, Iceland's most famous (and, it seems, somewhat revered) crime fiction author, will be present as the special guest of honor. It's clear that this is rare, and a point of pride; Yrsa and Ragnar tell me Arnaldur "never" goes to other festivals, but he is coming to theirs. Every crime fiction writer in Iceland will be there, they say, and I can feel the excited anticipation, even from this subdued duo. They'll have panels, one-on-one sessions, readings, interviews, and even some tours. Ragnar says they only got the idea for the festival this April, but already they've organized the whole of the crime fiction community to come together for this one weekend of events. I'm not even a crime fiction author but the energy sounds fantastic, and a bit of me wishes I could be here in November.

Talking with these authors, I get the sense that all the authors in Iceland know each other. Then again, I get the feeling that everyone in Iceland knows each other — or at the very least, they are far closer than six degrees of separation from one another. Three, at most, I'd guess. It is a small country. The upcoming crime festival sounds like it will be a spectacular party amongst close friends.

Crime fiction is quite popular in Iceland, which seems a bit of a paradox, considering that violent crime is almost nonexistent here. Maybe that's its appeal: It's a curiosity. Crime of any sort is rare, it seems, perhaps because Iceland has historically been such an egalitarian society. (The economic crash of 2008 did cause a "relatively minor up-tick in general crime," according to the U.S. Overseas Security Advisory Council.) This is not to say crime doesn't happen; it's just less common here than anywhere else I've been. Yrsa explains that crime fiction was not so popular until recently, but Arnaldur Indriðason changed all that. He started writing crime fiction about fifteen years ago, and broke out with his third novel. After that, she said, people realized that crime novels set in Iceland could be just as good as anywhere else, and a new trend was born. Now, writers like Arnaldur, Yrsa, Ragnar, and their colleagues are all part of a quickly growing "Nordic Noir" craze, fed in part by the success of Stieg Larsson (*The Girl with the Dragon Tattoo*).

Both writers have "day jobs": Ragnar currently works as a copyright lawyer, and Yrsa is an engineer. Does either have hopes to one day just be a writer? Absolutely not, they tell me. Having a day job, they agree, frees them from the stresses of writing full time. They don't feel the pressure to get a new book out every year, and their writing isn't hindered by worries about what will happen if the books don't succeed. I get the feeling Ragnar's day job feeds his writing, as well. As a lawyer, with friends in all areas of the law, situations that play out during the workday can lead to ideas and scenarios that he can then weave into his stories. For Yrsa, I suspect that her day job and her writing balance out her personality, a need for order combined with a thirst for excitement.

Ragnar, who has translated fourteen Agatha Christie novels into Icelandic (and once was the editor of agathachristie.net), undoubtedly learned a few tricks from the mystery master he translated. He's been writing his whole life, and it's obvious to me he's one of those people who can't not write. He indicates that he might be interested in exploring other genres, but crime, with its intrigue and red herrings and unexpected twists, is his true passion. It turns out Ragnar has been to Orcas Island, Washington. I tell him that's very much like the fictional Dogwinkle Island from my Wishing Rock books, and his gentle face breaks into a smile.

Yrsa, on the other hand, did not start out to be a writer. When her children were small, she was disappointed in the quality of children's books, so she started writing them herself. Then, I suppose the natural progression is from children's books to crime fiction, no? At any rate, she no longer writes for kids but instead gets her joy from writing things that make people's skin creep, writing both horror and crime. I'm intrigued by what must go through a person's mind in writing these books; my own books stay far away from anything scary or creepy, simply because my constitution can't handle that stuff. Some of the things she finds in her research research, she says, are horrible, almost more than she can take. I can only imagine how bad it must be. I don't press for details.

Neither Yrsa nor Ragnar writes every day, but they still put out about a book a year. The months of October through December, Ragnar explains, are usually devoted to book promotion and readings, gearing up for the Christmas rush. With a 100 percent literary rate, it's no surprise that books are popular Christmas gifts; in fact, there's a name for it: the Jolabokaflod, or "Christmas Book Flood." It's common for every person to receive at least a couple books, they tell me. With a proud literary history reaching back to medieval times in the Icelandic Sagas, literature holds a special place in Icelandic hearts. A writer's dream!

I'm interested, of course, in self-publishing. Yrsa squints slightly at the mention of the words. She says that publishing in Iceland is not like publishing elsewhere. Ragnar agrees, saying that if you have a manuscript, you can walk right into the publisher's office and give it to them. And they'll look it over. The only reason your book would not be published by a traditional publisher in Iceland, they say, is if your work is no good.

This isn't to say that no one tries. They still have the "vanity press," the old kind of self-publishing — where an author pays to have his or her book printed (at the same Icelandic printers, it should be noted, that print all the books by the "real" publishers), keeps a thousand copies in the basement or garage, and does the selling him/herself. Recently, an author was picked up by the Icelandic publishers after he self-published, and now his book is doing very well. I ask why, if a person can just walk into a publisher's office and get published, he hadn't done so? "He probably tried," Yrsa says. His book must not have been good enough, I gather. But he persisted and now is "official," like the rest.

When we get up to leave, I remember Ice Cream Ragnar's warm hug and for some reason — I don't know why — I decide this must be standard Icelandic protocol. Not wanting to seem aloof by offering just a handshake, I reach out to hug Yrsa. By her somewhat stiff response, I instantly realize this was not the thing to do. But I can't hug one and not the other, right? So I give Author Ragnar an awkward hug as well, inwardly laughing at myself for making assumptions. The Icelandic people are interesting. The outer shell is not necessarily warm at first, but every single person has been so kind. Mary Frances tells me there's a saying, that Icelanders will dance after drinking for two hours. (She also says that Icelanders generally show up to a party one hour late. I suppose this means that three hours after a party is scheduled to start, it really gets going!) We all warm up eventually, given the right conditions.

The author interview is over a little after noon, which leaves me just under an hour to walk the slightly more than a kilometer to City Hall ("Ráðhús") for my meeting with Jón Gnarr, mayor of Reykjavík. This is just the right amount of time, as it allows me time to get lost and re-found, or discover I've gone to the wrong place and make my way to the right place, or sit and have a cup of tea and look over my notes if all goes well. Yrsa walks me outside and points me in the direction of the road I should take. Her directions do not match the directions my map has suggested. I thank her, say goodbye to her and to Ragnar, who has also come outside, and mentally decide to follow the map. I pick my way back through the duck droppings outside Nordic House, down the road past the University of Iceland (fronted by a very utilitarian-looking large white box), to Tjörnin ("The Pond"), a picturesque little lake on which City Hall sits, in the center of Reykjavík. After checking the time (I am still plenty early), I stop to take in the city from this viewpoint. I'm struck, again, by how flat the city is. Quite walkable, which is a good point today.

I don't pause too long to ponder the pond and the city, though, because I do not want to leave the mayor waiting. I walk into City Hall and it occurs to me the place is as much a tourist attraction, at least on the ground floor, as it is a place of business. It's not like an office, really. People come here all the time who have no business to conduct here; in fact, there's a group of tourists here now, being led through the building by a woman carrying a flag on a stick. I'm not sure which country's flag it is, but it looks Scandinavian. The woman with the flag is walking mostly backward, calling out facts and information in some non-English language as she leads the people down the hall. I'm tempted to join in the group, just to see if they'd notice, but I am here on a mission.

I approach a woman at a desk. Seeing as she's the only person at any of the desks, I decide she's my gal.

"I'm here to see the mayor at 1:00," I say. "I'm not sure where I should go?"

She looks at me like she smells something funny. Well, I need to do laundry, sure, but I don't think I smell.

"You're here to see the mayor?" she asks, checking to see if she heard right.

"Yes. At 1:00. I know I'm early." It's about 12:40. "Is there a café around here?"

"Just at the corner there." I look, see some tables, nod.

"Then is this where I should come, when it's time?"

"Yes," she says.

I go to the café, which is on the side of the building that faces Tjörnin. The wall is made up of long panes of glass so visitors can enjoy the view of the pond. I sit for a bit and have a cup of tea, do some writing, watch the people go by, go over my questions. I have only half an hour with Jón Gnarr, but I have two pages, front and back, of potential questions. I want to make the best use of my time. I decide to skip all the political stuff — oddly enough, in interviewing a mayor — but I'm more interested in his life philosophy. Besides which, the two inevitably intertwine. Half an hour. Not nearly enough.

After about ten minutes, I'm getting antsy, so I head back to the desk. But no one is there! Where has the woman gone? No one is at the desk farther down the lobby, either. I don't see any official-looking people anywhere. I strain my neck to see around the woman's desk into the hallway behind it, but of course I can see nothing. Finally a trio of people appear by another desk, two of whom look like they might work here. They see me standing at the empty desk. I see them. We see each other. They don't make a move to come over. I stay where I am, not wanting to bother them and still hopeful that Desk Lady will return.

Finally, it is five minutes to one, and I don't want to show up late. I catch the attention of one of the men at the other desk. We walk toward each other, meet in the middle.

"Hi, I'm here to meet the mayor, and the woman who was at this desk told me I should come back here, but she's not here now."

"You're here to what?"

"Meet the mayor."

His attention is caught, though I'm not sure he's convinced. He gets on the phone. "What's your name?" he asks me.

"Pam Stucky," I say. "I'm supposed to meet with him at 1:00."

He calls someone, and an Icelandic conversation commences. He looks at me. "Pam?" he says.

"Yes," I say.

Icelandic conversation continues.

He hangs up.

"Follow me."

We go to the elevators, get on board. He swipes his card over the bank of elevator buttons. We must be going into a secure area! This is very exciting, in a way. I am excited, anyway. Easily impressed, I am.

I get off the elevator, and the man takes me to an office where an attractive young blonde woman is just getting up from her desk. The plaque on the door says "Unnur," so I know this is the woman I've been emailing with to arrange this meeting.

"It's so nice to meet you, finally," I say, and she agrees.

Then she leads me to a waiting area, with some couches where I am to wait. "He's running late," Unnur tells me.

"No problem," I say.

And I wait.

After a bit, "He's ten minutes away."

"No worries," I reassure. I have time.

Finally, about 1:20, Jón Gnarr appears in all his mayoral glory, with his associate Björn at his side. (For those who are interested, I believe this is Sigurður Björn Blöndal, political advisor.) Jón is handsome and tall, with spiky blond hair. He is dressed in "normal" clothes today. He isn't always. He famously dressed in drag for the Pride Parade one year. He owns (and wears) a beautiful bright pink suit. He dressed up as a Jedi knight to vote once. He is not a shy man when it comes to clothes.

Jón's background is fascinating. When he was young, he was misdiagnosed with severe mental retardation, suffered from dyslexia, and had learning disabilities (he still has ADHD). In his teens, he was in a punk band, and then later he got into radio and TV. Before becoming mayor, Jón was best known (and well known) for his comedy. He wrote shows for and starred in several seasons of the highly popular Icelandic show Fóstbræður ("Foster Brothers"). He was an anarchist and is a good friend of famous Icelandic singer Björk. He was not a politician.

Then came the economic crash of 2008. The people of Iceland were, to put it mildly, upset with their leaders for having gotten them into this mess. In the world of politics, anything and everything was suddenly possible.

In late 2009, Jón and a number of his friends and colleagues, all with no background in politics, formed "The Best Party." Jón threw his hat in the ring to run for mayor for the 2010 election. Initially, the campaign was somewhat of a joke, promising things like free towels at all the pools and a polar bear in every zoo, and further promising that they would break all their promises; the party's campaign slogan was "Afram allskonar!" or "Hooray for all kinds of things!" Nevertheless, the voters were interested in the idea of giving someone new a chance, and they already knew and loved Jón from his days on TV. The possibility that Jón might become mayor grew more serious.

Then, on May 29, 2010, The Best Party won 34.7 percent of the vote on the Reykjavík City Council, and Jón Gnarr was elected mayor.

He has been called the "World's Most Interesting Mayor," and I am eager to see if I agree.

Jón, Björn, and I all make introductions and shake hands, and I wonder if Björn will be joining us, to make sure I don't ask inappropriate questions or take unauthorized photos or something. But no, Björn exits left, while Jón escorts me to his office on the right.

I check to make sure Jón still has time to meet with me; if he has to save the world at 1:30 (at which time our interview was scheduled to end), I don't want to get in the way. He says all is fine. Unnur, who brought water to the office for us five or ten minutes ago, checks on us and closes the door behind herself. We begin.

I don't think I've mentioned this before: The Icelandic word for "yes" sounds a lot to me like "yow!" — complete with the exclamation point. "Yow!" or "Yeeoo!" I think it's actually "ja," like in German, but I'm not sure, and regardless, it sounds like "yow!" As

I introduce myself and start with the preliminaries, Jón is saying "Yow! Yow! Yow! Yow!"

At least it's not "Wikings."

I start out by explaining that I know I have a short time, and I'm not interested in asking questions about the campaign or things I already know the answers to. What I'm interested in, I tell him, is what drives people, people's passions, things like that. I point to the camera and explain that Unnur told me I can't video the interview, but I'm allowed to record sound, to get quotations right. With these preliminaries, we begin.

"It's been a little more than three years now that you've been in office," I say. "How have you and your views on life and the world changed in those three years?"

Jón's speech is measured, deliberate, his words meticulously chosen to ensure he picks the words that mean exactly what he is trying to say. "They have maybe not changed that much, but they have matured. I have gained a deeper understanding of things that have puzzled me, I've been puzzled by all my life," he says.

"Such as?"

"Human nature, for instance, and the very nature of the human being. All my life, or since I was, like, early teenage years, I've been very interested in how to organize the human community. I've been fascinated with democracy, and of course political theory, like Marxism, capitalism, and anarchism. So my views and my understanding of these things has matured, and I have deeper insight in it. All my life I've been just *fascinated* by people. I remember when I was very little, one of my first childhood memories, I grew up mostly with my mother and my grandmother and my mother's sisters. Women. Mostly women. I remember when I was like six or seven, I just loved to be with my mother and her sisters. Just watching them and observing them and listening to them. And I was quite sure that these people were the most fascinating people in the world. In my opinion. I was sure, there was no doubt, these four women, they are probably the most intelligent, beautiful, and fantastic people."

"Did you ever tell them that?"

"No, no I didn't, not until later. They're all dead now. Yeah, and just trying to understand why people behave how they behave, what motivates them, what's their drive, why do they respond in different ways. I've been quite taken, also, by the words that people use."

This is interesting, because it's evident that he himself picks his words thoughtfully. I don't know if it's a language issue — he speaks English fluently, but possibly he's not as comfortable in it as he is in Icelandic — or if he simply has an appreciation for the subtle nuances and different meanings of similar words, and wants to be sure he chooses the precise words he wants. Or, being in the public eye, maybe he's very aware of being quoted (or misquoted), and he wants to make sure he says what he means to say. His speaking is sometimes slow, but not drawn out; it has an aura of carefully chosen language.

I tell him he sounds like a writer, that these things are exactly why I write.

"I've always thought a lot about why people choose specific and different words, and the use of language. I think that my drive in whatever I've been doing is just to observe people, and study people. It's always people study for me. Like, through comedy. It's been like a scientific project, through comedy, for me, studying 'Why do people laugh? What is it?' When I'm combining words like in stand-up, I was a stand-up comedian, and I really enjoyed being on stage and just watching people and reading their faces and their body language and making them laugh and making them nervous, and stuff like that."

"Just to see what would happen?"

"Yeah, yeah, yeah. I had it as a goal to also gain physical control over people through comedy."

"Physical control through comedy?" I ask for clarification.

"Yeah. I could. Like, making people cry. And even, I have been successful at that, making them piss their pants."

We laugh. "We all have to have a goal," I say.

"People have admitted to me that 'when you did this, I …'"

"'… I let go.'"

He chuckles. "Yeah. So when I went into politics, decided to interfere and come up with this initiative and get involved with politics, it was out of people love. I wanted to get myself into this world, to experience people and communication and this type of communication. I think if I had had a healthy normal upbringing and education, I think I would automatically have become an anthropologist, probably."

"Anthropologist?"

"Yes."

"You also have an interest in neuroscience," I say. I read that somewhere once, and his interest in neuroscience is on my list of questions.

"Yeah. I'm fascinated … and that is also to do with people …"

"Digging in there. Digging internally or externally. Discovery. Curiosity."

"Yeah, yeah. Yeah, probably an anthropologist, or even a neuroscientist. Neuroscientists are, in my opinion now, I think it's the…." Jón searches a bit for the word he wants; comes up with, "… it's the coolest job that anyone could have, to be a neuroscientist. For me, it's like being an astronaut. It's like something …"

"A new world."

"Yes, it's a new world, it's so fascinating, and with all the new technology we have now, to be able to examine and look at the brain in a way we've never been able to do before."

"I heard that you did an interview last week in which you said you're not going to run again. If that is the truth, would you want to be a neuroscientist or anthropologist? Or what would you want to do after this year has taken its course?"

"No, I think I would not make a good neuroscientist if I started now. I have no college degree or anything, so I'd have to start from scratch, and that's boring, and I don't want to do that. If I had the opportunity of enrolling into a university, I would like to study anthropology. I have friends who are anthropologists and I can just spend hours and hours with them, picking their brains about different things. But yow!, yeah, the word I was looking for when I said 'cool job' was a 'cool field of work.'"

"You once said your only goal is to make people happy. Do you think you've succeeded in your time as mayor in making people happy, and are you happy?"

"Yeah, I would consider myself to be an extremely happy person. Impatient, maybe, but happy. I'm quite happy to exist. To have had the opportunity to be born and be alive, and I want to get as much experience from this time as possible. I really enjoy to see people happy. That's something that gives me some sort of fulfillment, to see people happy. As I said, one of my greatest passions in life was my stand-up [comedy]. Before I had a show, I would sit backstage, and I would listen to the sound of people coming in, entering. Yeah, just the sound of it, I enjoyed it. I would just sit alone, I didn't want to be disturbed, I didn't want to have any conversations with anybody, I just wanted to be alone and listen to people coming in. And then directly afterwards, I went into the same place, and listened to people go out, and just feel the difference of the energy, just hearing people having conversations, laughing, you know, it was a totally different energy."

"You'd made a change in the world."

"YES," he says emphatically. "And that gave me an enormous fulfillment. And even sentimental. Quite sentimental."

"Yeah, I can see, I can imagine that. I'm getting a little teary-eyed thinking about it. That's powerful." Well, I was. What can I say. I'm an emotional being.

"Yes. Yeah. And it has also a lot to do with my passion for people and communication. I mean the human animal is the most fascinating species ever to exist and the human brain is the most fascinating item in the history of the world. I really like reading books on the topic, like Malcolm Gladwell…"

I try to remember another author on happiness, but fail.

Jón continues. "I read a very interesting book, *The Geography of Bliss* by Eric Weiner. It's a very good book. He writes a chapter on Iceland, and happiness, and stuff like that."

I'm familiar with the book, having read it myself. "Do you agree with him on the assessment of Iceland as one of the happiest places; do you think that's true?" I ask.

He pauses to consider. "I don't know. I was a bit skeptical on the chapter on Iceland. I enjoyed other chapters more. It's very complex. Of course I'm fascinated with … I've had the privilege of being born here, which is a total coincidence because I could so easily have been born somewhere else. I had the privilege of being born here in quite a small community in this isolated island with its remarkable history. Happiness has a lot to do with the Icelandic mentality. It's very seasonal. We are so dependent on the seasons and on nature. To be able to survive here on this island, and have a happy, normal life, you have to have certain qualities. You have to be very adaptive, and it's essential to be positive. Otherwise you'd just go mad. You have to have almost insane positivity, and always see the positive. I think it's a part of the Icelandic mentality. If you're among a group of Icelanders, say at some event like a birthday or some gathering, and you complain about the weather, for instance: 'Woah. What crap weather we've been having.' Nobody will agree."

"Really?"

"No. People will say, like, 'What do you mean? The weather has been okay,' and 'There's no such thing as bad weather, only bad clothing.' They have sayings and stuff. So we are extremely positive. And we even have a saying in Icelandic: 'Þetta reddast.'"

"I know that one!" I say with delight, remembering what Ice Cream Ragnar told me. "Everything will work out."

Jón nods. "Everything's going to work out. No matter how bad things are, and how hopeless everything seems, everybody will be saying, 'Yeah, þetta reddast. It's going to be okay.' And that's been so big a part of our history. You know, you build a house and it crumbles in the next earthquake. And your crops will fail because maybe the summer never comes. We have years without summer, you know. This is so important when you're trying to understand the mentality of the people who live here. And also this adaptiveness, to be able to adapt to ever-changing situations, circumstances."

"Would you say resilience, as well?"

"Yeah, very resilient. And opportunistic. Because that's been a vital part of survival, to see the opportunities, and seize them. And it all depends on nature and it all depends on the weather. I also think that plays a key role in the importance of literature, too, with this nation, and storytelling. Because that's what people did in the dark winter months. You know, what were you supposed to do? It was dark, months and months and months of darkness, and that's an opportunity to tell stories, to be a storyteller."

Jón tracks back to the original question of happiness. "I mean, happiness is a state of mind. Like Eric Weiner says in his book, Iceland scores high on the happy list, and why, in a country where you don't see what they have to be happy about, why are they so happy, when they seem to have not so much to be happy about? It's like a state of mind. It's like, I mean, yeah, but in fact life has always been very hard here, and yeah, quite hard and quite tough sometimes."

"Speaking of storytelling," I say, "you're writing a book. Tell me about that."

I follow Jón on Facebook, and earlier in the year he'd posted that he was going to write a book about his experiences as mayor, which he was going to title *Listen Carefully and Then Repeat*. I ask him about the book he's writing, and he tells me it's done. I'm confused, because I know how long it takes to write a book, and he can't possibly have finished? But he tells me the book is being published in Germany (and in German), and is titled *Hören Sie gut zu und wiederholen Sie!!!* which does, in fact, translate to, "listen carefully and then repeat." He says it's based on his attempt to learn German on Linguaphone, a self-study language course that's available on CDs.

A German publisher contacted him, he says. "They wanted me to write a book on my experience as mayor and my theories on life and the universe and everything."

"So to speak," I say. I recognize the Douglas Adams reference because I am savvy like that. We laugh in solidarity.

"Yeah, so I did that, and I wrote a book, it's called, *Hören Sie gut zu und wiederholen Sie!!!* It's a line from my German Linguaphone, when I tried to learn German. When I was doing stand-up, I used to travel around, and I liked to travel in my car, to drive. I can't stand music, and I never have listened to music."

At this point, Unnar comes in to let us know we need to wrap up our interview soon. Already? It has gone so fast and I have so much more to ask!

When she's gone again, Jón repeats: "I can't stand music, and I have never listened to music."

This is familiar; I've read about this in my research on him. "I heard your brain is oversensitive?" I say.

"Yes, it's like a hypersensitivity thing or something. I get uncomfortable with music."

"Too much stimulation."

"Yes. I can tolerate like one song, two songs, maybe, and then I get physical discomfort, like it's hard to breathe. But I like the spoken word. I listen to spoken words. I really like audio books and podcasts, I like to listen to all of This American Life, Radio Lab, really good talk radio, informative and entertaining at the same time. And I used to drive, my long drives, could be hours and hours of driving, and always in total silence. I was interested in learning German, so I bought a German Linguaphone, and I thought it was a great idea, just have a Linguaphone playing in the car, and then all of a sudden I would know German! But no, it's just boring conversations. Linguaphone conversations are so boring. I just spaced out of it. But I always heard this 'Hören Sie gut zu und wiederholen Sie!!!' So that's about the only thing I learned."

And with that, Unnur came in again to let us know it was time for me to go.

I gather my things and get up to leave, as Unnur is already speeding Jón along in preparations for his next appointment. "I'm going to go bike for cancer now," he says, holding up a bright yellow biking shirt Unnur has given him to change into. It occurs to me that this man must have a rather insane schedule; he is well liked and sought out, and undoubtedly he is in demand every minute of every very long day. I don't correct him by saying, "I assume you mean you're going to bike *against* cancer." Instead I thank both Jón and Unnur again for their time and help, and head out to the next interview. Three interviews down (well, two interviews, three people), one to go.

On my way out of City Hall, I am very tempted to take a picture of the snyrting signs. All through this whole trip I've been wanting to take a picture of the word "snyrting" next to the men's and ladies' rooms, but I feel a bit silly doing so. The snyrting sign here at City Hall is particularly artistic, somehow, and I am drawn to it. But alas, there are a number of people in the café, across from the snyrting, and I let this prevent me from taking a picture. After all, I don't really need a picture of a sign that says "snyrting" any more than my grandparents needed the eighteen thousandth picture of their roses. It was just a thing to do. I exit, knowing the snyrting will remain nothing but a memory.

The interview with Jón has left me buoyant. Such a great conversation and an interesting person. I never did learn whether he intends to run for office again, and from our conversation I couldn't guess. (Personally, I wonder if Björn, the political advisor who was with Jón when he arrived, might run.) Jón is certainly not your average politician. He seems far more interested in doing what is right than in doing what would benefit Jón Gnarr, and the two are not always somehow mysteriously one and the same, as they seem to be sometimes with other politicians. He is not afraid to admit when he doesn't know something, or to seek more information to help him make decisions. At the same time, I suspect the mundanity of politics and government can't keep him interested for too long. I'm reminded of Plato's idea of the "Philosopher King" — that the person who is best suited to lead the people is usually the least interested in the job. In my opinion, any government would be lucky to have a person like Jón at the helm. He is a refreshing light of honesty and reality. It was a delight to talk with him and I'm sad it ended so soon. Maybe one day our paths will cross again.

On to the last interview of the day. Last Monday (the Monday after the Saturday the mayor of Akureyri and I were originally scheduled to meet), an ambulance plane crashed on a race track near Akureyri, killing two and injuring the third person on board. Akureyri is home to only about eighteen thousand people, and most people know or at least know of each other. Mayor Eiríkur Björn Björgvinsson has spent the week both grieving lost friends, and helping his city and its people cope with the loss, and he is tired. Still, he graciously makes time to meet with me while he's in Reykjavík on other business.

We meet in the Hotel Borg, across from parliament and overlooking the quaint and compact Austurvöllur Square, with its giant statue of Jón Sigurdsson, who led Iceland to its independence from Denmark just a few decades ago. (I can't help but wonder if people are assimilated at Hotel Borg. Another Star Trek joke. What can I say, "borg" comes up a lot in Iceland — it means "city.")

Eiríkur strides into the hotel, tall and lithe, trim, shape of a basketball player, perhaps. As it turns out, my assessment is not far off: Eiríkur started his career as a sports teacher, and served as a sports director in Egilsstaðir in east Iceland (on the Lagarfljót river — where the worm is!) for two years before he was approached by the people of Egilsstaðir to run for mayor there. He ran, won, and served two four-year terms before Akureyri came calling after the economic crash of 2008. He was elected mayor of Akureyri in 2010 (the same year Jón Gnarr was elected mayor of Reykjavík; all mayoral races are decided in the same years, apparently), and says, "If the people want me to continue [for another term], I will serve." The next elections will be held in May 2014.

Eiríkur loves being mayor because it gives him the chance to have influence and share good ideas. He likes to "serve people, be a part of helping people, be a part of creating things, of building community," he says. Since the crash of 2008, life has been difficult for everyone. "It's so important to stabilize," he says, and to continue to build.

Eiríkur is clearly passionate about Akureyri and the north. From the start his pride shows in the way he advocates for the region and its people, and perhaps a slight bit in the way he declines to see any negatives about the area. I'm reminded of the intense Icelandic positivity Jón Gnarr was talking about — always seeing the good side. I see now why Eiríkur worked so hard to make this interview happen after it fell through the first time: Reykjavík usually gets the accolades and the ink; Eiríkur wants to be sure the north, his region and his people, get their due time in the spotlight. He explains that Akureyri is "more conservative politically and morally" than Reykjavík, and is strong with a tremendous history, while at the same time it is building into a modern society. He proudly rattles off the names of numerous famous Akureyrians and the corresponding museums dedicated to them in his city, including a memorial museum dedicated to poet Davíð Stefánsson, and Nonnahús or Nonni House, childhood home of writer Jón Sveinsson — so many places to visit to learn about the people and the place. To get a real sense of the area, he says, a visitor should plan to spend at least a week in the north, with Akureyri as a base. "It's important to make people know that they have this area for day tourism," he says. "We have all the facilities you need."

I ask, what does Akureyri have to teach the world; what does Akureyri do better than anyone? "Being ourselves," he says. "We haven't changed for decades. We're a modern country but we still have the sagas, our heritage. We believe in ourselves, and we are independent." We discuss the hearts Akureyri is famous for, that I'd seen in the stoplights up on the hill. After the economic crash of 2008, he explains, the people of Akureyri asked themselves, what can we do to help people feel better again? One answer was the hearts. Eiríkur says there's even a mountain across from town where lights have been installed into the hillside, in the shape of a heart. The lights form an enormous heart that is on display in the winter months, and for one weekend at the end of August.

"The Heart of the North," I suggest, and Eiríkur smiles at the idea.

"The Heart of the North," he repeats. "When I have the opportunity to tell people, I'm so proud of how people in Akureyri are, how friendly they are. The hospitality of the people in Akureyri is unbelievable," he says, "Akureyri is strong."

On the other end of the spectrum, what could Akureyri and Iceland stand to learn? He says they may need to "learn to be a part of the global world," he says. "The people living on this planet are one family."

I do discuss with Eiríkur my experience on the Diamond Circle, my frustration over the 864 road, and the fact that I wouldn't send anyone over it without warning. I ask about infrastructure, whether it's too soon to be working to promote the Diamond Circle before good roads are in place. Eiríkur explains that I took the wrong road to Dettifoss; I should have taken the 862 north from the Ring Road. The complication, of course, is that to avoid 864 I either have to make two large arcs, one northern arc out to Ásbyrgi and back, and then a southern arc to Dettifoss and back, which is a lot of backtracking, and not really in line with the promoted idea of a "circle." Further, because I couldn't drive on the northern part of the 862 I missed some sites I really wanted to see. Again I see the doggedly positive attitude at work. Eiríkur reiterates that Akureyri has much to offer, many spectacular sites and wonderful people, despite any challenges, and assures me that the infrastructure of Akureyri is very strong indeed in businesses and services. Although I do leave our conversation thinking that a dose of practicality is critical if the Diamond Circle and tourism in the north hope to grow, I appreciate the passion Eiríkur has for Akureyri, its people, and the region.

I walk back to Mary Frances's, not getting lost once, and arrive just before she and her family get home. We have dinner and again spend the evening chatting and watching the kids' favorite movies on TV. Mary Frances's husband, a journalist, has an assignment to write an editorial, so we toss around ideas for topics. Half-jokingly, he suggests he could write about the pressure on Icelanders with American spouses to have pets. While dogs are no longer banned in Reykjavik, and I've seen a good number of people out walking dogs, I gather that many Icelanders have not yet fully bought into the idea of house pets. Yet about six out of ten Americans have pets. Marry an Icelander to an American, and apparently the house pet conversation often comes up.

We are once again in bed before the sun is. I've definitely noticed the difference in the time of sunset between the far west coast and Reykjavík, and with such a wide swing from almost 24 hours of daylight in summer to almost 24 hours of dark in winter, the shift happens quickly. Sunset comes about six and a half minutes earlier each day here, in contrast to about just under three and a half minutes earlier in Seattle. In Iceland, you grab the daylight while you can. It is going fast.

Pride

Saturday, August 10, 2013

It's Pride Day. August 6 through 11 is Gay Pride "weekend" this year, but the big event is the Reykjavík Pride Parade, which is today. One of Mary Frances's friends works for a volunteer organization, and has put out a call looking for people to help staff the parade. Mary Frances and I have agreed to help. After all, what better way to understand a city, get its pulse, than to be a part of its second largest annual event?

Ice Cream Ragnar and I had discussed the Pride Parade and weekend. He said that it wasn't even that long ago that Iceland's attitude toward the LGBT community was leaning toward completely intolerant. As he put it, though, people started to realize that tolerance was a much better idea, and now the city fully embraces the community and this parade. He said that while many cities' pride parades have turned into giant parties with alcohol and reckless rowdiness, in Reykjavík people started bringing their children, their parents, everyone, and now the parade has become a huge family event. Each year, he told me, 100,000 people of all ages and backgrounds will attend the event — which, for a city with a population around 200,000 (including the surrounding areas) and a country with a population around 320,000, is enormous.

It sounds like a can't-miss event. We're in.

(For the record, Reykjavík's — and Iceland's — biggest event is "Menningarnótt" or "Culture Night," held in late August. The Pride Parade says "up to" 100,000 people enjoy the event every year, and Menningarnótt states that it brings in "more than" 100,000 people, so the attendance seems fairly close, but Menningarnótt is generally listed as being bigger. As I understand it, Menningarnótt usually coincides with the Reykjavík marathon. Celebrations range from musical and dance performances to exhibitions and fairs, capped off with fireworks at midnight. It sounds like it might be one of those events that is timed like Thanksgiving in the U.S. — that is, not on the same day every year and not even always on the same weekend of the month. In some places I've read it's the third weekend in August; other sources say it's the first Saturday after August 18. If you plan to attend, just be sure you get the right date!)

Mary Frances and I start our Pride morning with a hike to the bus station, where we will meet up with the organizers and the other volunteers. We will serve as security; our assignment will be to stand in a line at the parade and keep people from going over the line. We feel this is vital to the safety of the people. Perhaps if the job were truly critical to the safety of the city, they wouldn't leave it to random volunteers, but we feel quite important nonetheless.

Rather than walking me straight to the bus station, though, Mary Frances decides I first must have the one delicacy for which Reykjavík is most famous. Not fermented shark, thank goodness. No, Reykjavík is famous for hot dogs; specifically, hot dogs from Bæjarins Beztu Pylsur ("Town's Best Hot Dog"), a hot dog stand somewhat near the end of the parade route. It was even once voted the best hot dog in Europe, which makes me wonder if bratwurst was included in that? Because if so, I wonder how Germany felt about it. Anyway, we go to the stand and there is no line at all, which Mary Frances finds amazing. I order "one with everything" (in Icelandic, "eina með öllu"), as I'm instructed to do. This includes a dog of pork, beef, and lamb, slathered with relish, ketchup, mustard, onion, perhaps a few other things. The hot dog is, in fact, quite good. Not mind-blowingly effervescently good, but it's a good dog, with a nice snap to the casing when you bite down and a tasty mix of condiments. I consume what is sometimes called "Iceland's national food," and then we head on to the bus station.

When we arrive, we see other people milling about aimlessly, looking like volunteers waiting to be told what to do, so we know we're in the right place. Then we see some people wearing bright orange safety vests. The writing on the back is in Icelandic, but Mary Frances tells me the vests say things like "Parade Organizer" and "Manager" and such. We are very hopeful that we get to wear bright orange safety vests, too.

I decide I might not have another chance to use a restroom for a while, so I head to the bus station WC. Inside, the light is blue. I know from watching Rick Steves on PBS that this means they're trying to discourage drug users from using the bathroom to shoot up; apparently you can't find your veins in blue light. Luckily, all I needed to do was pee.

When I come back out, things are already happening. We do, in fact, get our own bright orange vests. Ours say, in English, "Reykjavík Pride Staff." I'm proud already, just wearing it.

As part of our "payment" for helping out today, we get lunch vouchers for soup and a roll from the bus station café. I choose mushroom soup over fish soup. It is delicious and filling. We sit with another volunteer, a young man who is making his way around the world as a volunteer, taking on various volunteer opportunities as he can find them, that provide him with room and board and a chance to make a difference. He just arrived in Reykjavík last week, and this is his first volunteer opportunity.

Mary Frances explains that volunteering is not a big thing in Iceland, she has found. Here, they believe if you're doing a job you should be paid for it. She says this is in part because of what the Icelanders call "vinnuskóki," which translates to "work school"; every summer from the time they are about fifteen, Icelanders are paid by the municipality to work, usually in gardens or the post office or something like that, so they are used to being paid for their work. It fascinates me to see, once again, the various ways people organize themselves. In Iceland, the tax rate is around fifty percent, but your health care and education are provided. Mary Frances got her Master's degree here, and the tax return from the one year she worked between undergrad and grad school covered her tuition. When she went to the hospital to give birth, the parking ticket she got for parking illegally was higher than the cost of her delivery — and the parking ticket was only about $25. But on the other side, volunteering isn't something that is valued in this culture, which is a huge contrast to what I'm used to. I'm not saying either way is right or wrong. It's just interesting to see the different ways we do things. There isn't always an obvious answer, and it's so valuable to be exposed to other approaches; there's always something we can learn.

Bellies full of soup and bread, we walk en masse as a giant swarm of orange to the parade route. The parade will start at Vatnsmýrarvegur, by the bus station (BSÍ), and end at the outdoor stage by the park, Arnarhóll. We are stationed along one side of the route on the road named Sóleyjargata. Volunteers spread out about fifty feet from each other along the route, but while we're waiting for the parade to start, Mary Frances and I (as well as other people volunteering in groups) inch toward each other to allow for easier chatting.

It becomes my unspoken but valiant mission to greet everyone who walks by with a cheerful, "Hello!" and often, "How are you today?" to see how many people I can get to smile. Mary Frances tells me this forced cheerfulness is very American of me, but she joins in as well. And people do respond. Individuals, couples of all gender pairings, families with children, people of all ages pass us by on their way to find the perfect spot along the route from which to watch the parade. Many are decked out in rainbow colors, some from head to toe, others with just a lei or hat. Everyone is in the mood to celebrate, and our greetings bring out smiles and brief conversations of cheer.

But then, the parade begins, and Mary Frances and I are all business. This is serious, people.

A line has been chalked on the sidewalk along the route, about three feet in from the street's edge. The volunteer organizer came by earlier with a long ribbon of caution tape, threading it from volunteer to volunteer. Our job is to Keep People Behind the Line. We are to do this firmly but kindly. We have practiced. "Sir, do you mind stepping behind the line?" "Excuse me, miss, behind the line, please," with a smile. But now, it's Go Time. The parade is about to begin. Will all our practice have prepared us for this monumental task?

It's an interesting thing, lines. And rules. And rules about lines. They're so arbitrary, yet they help maintain fairness and order. People who step over the line make it harder for people who are following the line rules to see, and it's my job to gently nudge people back. While I realize this is not life and death, I also understand the purpose of the line, so I do my best. Most people comply, and no one complains.

The front of the parade, for which people have been straining their necks and testing the line limits, finally approaches our stretch of the route. My new best friend, Jón Gnarr, is in the lead float, dressed in the women's national Icelandic costume.

He neither sees nor waves at me, but I'm nonplussed. I assume he didn't want the world to know how close we've become, so quickly. In fact, I'd assume he might even be a little intimidated by how great our interview was, and a little shy about waving at me. He's like that. A total introvert.

And thus the parade continues with all the usual floats, plus a few related to the specific politics of the day. Music emanates loudly from the floats, and the floats themselves bounce with the force of many people jumping and dancing with joy. People on the sidelines cheer and wave, and stay more or less behind the line. Reykjavík Pride Parade 2013 begins and parades and ends, and from my standpoint, right on the line, it was a great, festive success.

But by now Mary Frances and I have been standing for hours. We have not sat down since the bus station; nor have we had food nor water. Caught in an impenetrable flow of people, we follow along with the stream until we can break away a little before the park. We walk the long way around the park to try to escape the crowds, which gives us a great view of the grassy expanse and the multitudes of people setting up on the lawn, getting ready for the music. The crowd is massive. I am in awe of the number of people here, of all ages. It truly is a family event.

We keep walking and eventually find ourselves once again by the hot dog stand. In great contrast to this morning, this afternoon the line is enormous — and what's more, they've even brought in a second hot dog stand to help serve the hungry throng. By rough count, we estimate more than one hundred fifty people are waiting in the two lines combined. That is one popular dog.

On our walk back to her home, Mary Frances mentions that you can walk around in Reykjavík with your beer in hand, right there in the street, and it's totally legal. Therefore, it becomes an imperative that we stop by the nearest Vínbúðin and pick something up to carry (and drink) as we walk. When we get there, the lines are almost as bad as at the hot dog stand. Security officers are letting people inside in groups, so as to avoid having too many people in the store at once. We enter at the very end of the next group — I rush forward so as not to be the first part of the group after us instead. Mary Frances finds a beer and I find a lime drink of some sort, and we are on our way.

Back at Mary Frances's house and finally, finally sitting, we are too exhausted to make dinner. I offer to buy pizza for the family, and Mary Frances orders. When the pizza guy arrives, I hand him my credit card, and then realize I don't know tipping etiquette.

Mary Frances isn't sure, either. They don't order out a lot.

So I ask the pizza guy. "Do I tip you?"

I was expecting to hear, "Yes." Once when I was in another country where I'd heard people don't tip, I'd asked the same thing at a bar. The server had told me they wouldn't refuse it, which left me in sort of an awkward place and still not quite understanding protocol.

But Pizza Guy tells me, flat out, "No."

"Are you sure?" I ask.

"Yes, you don't tip."

And so I didn't tip. I never, ever really feel comfortable not tipping, and I don't know if it's deliveries in Iceland where you don't tip, or pizza delivery only, or this guy, or this particular place, or all of Iceland, but I was grateful for his honesty.

The pizza was delicious.

After dinner, I check email only to discover I'm in demand. An Icelandic journalist, from Morgunblaðið, which she says is "Iceland's biggest news-site," has heard about me and my travels, and wants to interview me. What?! I am shocked and amazed and delighted. Remember that three degrees of separation in Iceland I was talking about? Somehow, I have become a part of it. This journalist, Una Sighvatsdóttir, wants to do a phone interview me, "today or tomorrow."

I look at the time stamp of the email. She sent it this morning and it's now evening. Am I too late? Yes, I want to do an interview! Yes! But am I too late? I quickly send off a reply and cross my fingers. I leave tomorrow, Sunday. It's tomorrow or never.

I tidy up my luggage a bit, packing up anything I won't need anymore and leaving out what I will. We are in bed early. It's been a long but good day.

Interview and Home

Sunday, August 11, 2013

Sunday dawns bright, sunny, and gorgeous. I sigh, thinking it would have been lovely to have had bright, sunny, gorgeous weather on the days I wasn't leaving the country. Still, that's what you get in Iceland. You can certainly hope for better, but if you expect or plan on better you could find yourself disappointed. Mary Frances tells me there are about ten good days in summer. That may be an exaggeration, but it also may not. The last few days here have been overcast and gray, but today the sun is out, the sky is blue, the air is full of promise. It would be the perfect day to head out on a walk of the town and see all the tourist spots I missed in the last few days, the church, the concert hall, that Sun Voyager sculpture by the sea, the town walk, all of it. Everyone who comes to Reykjavík seems to go to the top of Hallgrímskirkja and take a picture of Reykjavík with the "miniature" feature on their cameras, making the town look like a little mini village. I'd meant to do that, but didn't have time. On trips, there's never enough time, and it goes so fast. The best we can do is make the time we have count, and I know I've done that.

Una Sighvatsdóttir from the news-site emailed me first thing this morning, and we've arranged that she'll call me at 11 a.m. to interview me. After some back-and-forth, we figured out that one of the authors I interviewed told someone about me and my travels and my book, who told someone else, who told someone else, who told Una. I'm quite amused by how fast news travels here, and amazed that my travels are of interest.

I'm nervous. I'm never comfortable being on the interview end of an interview. I know first-hand how inane people can sound in an interview when it's written down, and I'm not talking about other people; I'm talking about me. When I was in college, I was the editor of the school newspaper my junior year. I then ran for student government, and won, so I became a story for the paper. I sat with a reporter who interviewed me, and I watched carefully as he wrote my words down, so I know that what he wrote is what I said. When the story came out, though, I didn't recognize my own words at all. "Did I really say that?!" I thought, but having watched the reporter take notes, and knowing his journalistic integrity, I knew I must have. That was just a college newspaper. This is "Iceland's biggest news-site." When I get nervous, there's no telling what words will come out of my mouth. "Please don't sound like an idiot, Pam," I say to myself. "Please think before you speak."

Una calls, and either the interview isn't very long or because I'm nervous it flies by. She asks about my writing, why I'm here, what I'm writing about, what I think about the country. I discuss with her the beautiful country, the wonderful, warm people, and the need for Iceland to look at its infrastructure if it hopes to increase tourism.

At this last bit, Una replies, "Yes." Then a pause. "You noticed that?"

She asks whether I have any suggestions on how to deal with this. I say I'm no expert, and it's a difficult problem, but that one thing Iceland needs to do while building infrastructure is be sure to manage expectations, so people don't come here with high hopes and leave disappointed because of frustration over roads or crowds or weather.

We chat a bit more, and then she asks where people might buy my book once it's out. "We Icelanders love to read about ourselves," she laughs.

I list for her my website and the various sites where this book will be available. She thanks me and I thank her, and that's that.

The interview will be in Icelandic, as the site is Icelandic-only. I may not even be able to read it, but I hope at the very least I sounded intelligent.

With that, I pack up the last of my belongings, tuck my computer into the carry-on for easy access at the security gate at the airport, return Mary Frances's keys, pack my jacket away. It's warm back home so I'm dressed in layers so as not to suffocate when I step off the plane in Seattle. It's time to leave.

Mary Frances drives me to the bus station, where I buy a ticket and hop on the airport bus. It's nearly twenty minutes before the bus is scheduled to leave, but already it's almost full. The seat I grab at the back is one of only three left. Two more people get on the bus, filling it, and with no reason to wait until the time it's scheduled to leave, we're on our way early. The bus has WiFi, so I quickly text home, then sit and watch the first part of my trip go by in reverse. After a while, I think that by now we should be just about directly north of Blue Lagoon. I look out the window and sure enough, there it is, steaming out of the earth five miles away with nothing between it and me. Iceland: vast, barren, complex, dramatic, magnificent, gorgeous, ever changing, ever positive, ever hopeful.

And that's it. I made it all the way around the country, more or less. I didn't crash my car. I didn't drive off an edge. I only caused two power outages and set off one fire alarm. I met so many wonderful people. I thought about stuff. That sounds trite, but it matters. Having our world views expanded every now and then, recognizing that there's a lot we don't know, that's important. I talked to authors and mayors and students and business owners and visitor centre employees and natives and transplants. I didn't see or do nearly enough. I'm left, as always at the end of a trip, eager to get home but at the same time already planning my trip back. There's the Westfjords, you see, I didn't see them, and I must. And Þingvellir, I want to go back and hike aimlessly for hours, and snorkel in the tectonic rift at Silfra. And the interior, the highlands, whatever you call it, I didn't even touch that. Landmannalaugar, Fjaðrárgljúfur Canyon. More waterfalls. More pools. A good walk around Reykjavík. The far northeast. Back to Skagaströnd and the multitudes of little villages in the northwest.

Iceland, I'll be back.

In the Rear View Mirror

Looking Back

On any trip, it's sometimes hard to see the forest for the trees. You're caught up in what's happening day to day — making sure you get to the gas station in time to pay with your non-chip-and-PIN card, calculating exactly how much farther you can drive on gravel roads before you go insane, wondering whether you have enough underwear to get you through the rest of the trip — and you lose sight of the forest. Metaphorically speaking of course, if we're talking about Iceland.

It's only upon returning home that the big picture really starts to come into focus. That's what this section is about.

Would I visit Iceland again?

What would I change about itinerary?

What would I tell people who want to go there?

I was so intrigued by Una's response when I suggested Iceland needed to look at its infrastructure if it wants to increase tourism. Her, "Yes…. You noticed that?" was amusing, but at the same time, telling. I think this is a challenge that Icelanders may be aware of, but it seemed it might be a surprise, at least to some, that it's evident to tourists as well. When Una asked for my suggestions for how to fix this problem, I was a little flustered. I am neither politician nor economist, and I know the issues are complex. I don't want to suggest that I have the answers, by any means. But one thing I love about Icelanders is that they have such an open approach to discussion. They don't immediately take sides and close down. They are interested in ideas and in communicating and debating, and are open to changing course when necessary. While deeply rooted in their country and their traditions, they are not tied to one view of "right," and are open to adapting as the situation requires. This, I think, is one of the country's people's great strengths, and something that in the long run will help them thrive despite whatever setbacks they may face (and, in fact, has already done so).

In reading articles about Iceland lately, and following Icelandic and Iceland-interested people online, I see I'm not the only one who has noticed these challenges of infrastructure. Just as with Visitor Centre Guy, who commented that there's not much room for more tourists, many people feel that Iceland has reached a tourism saturation point. And yet, people are talking about the current tourism gold rush in Iceland. Everyone wants a piece of this lucrative pie. But what happens with a gold rush? Most people come up empty-handed. If Iceland is already "full," but yet people are still courting more and more tourists to visit, what happens when those visitors get there? Frustration over the lack of roads and facilities; disappointment that the serene, isolated Iceland they were hoping for is, instead, a cattle-rush of people all going to the same sites. The right hand needs to talk to the left, as the saying goes. If one group is inviting people to come visit, but the other hasn't gotten the house ready for the party, there's trouble ahead.

It does sound like Iceland wants to continue to build tourism, and that's the assumption I'm going with. The number one challenge, then, is finding a balance in preserving the Iceland that people come to see, while at the same time expanding and improving the access and opportunities to see it. Right now, there's an influx of tourists, but not enough places for them all to go. Iceland needs to find ways to spread those people out over more sites, and that means building more and better roads, and clean, accessible facilities. If you are inviting the world to come visit, but there's nowhere for them to go when they get there because everything is already spilling over with other tourists, then people will start driving off into places they're not supposed to go. I'd read about the fragile landscape and how one person driving off-road can damage the land for years, and that seemed extreme — until I saw it. As I mentioned earlier in this book, out in the middle of nowhere, I saw two tire tracks carved into land and time, trailing off into the distance. In contrast, what if you created a better infrastructure, gave people safe roads to remote places? In my non-scientific view, people will stay on the trail … if you give them a trail to stay on. The whole country doesn't have to be developed — and shouldn't. A little will go a long way, in my opinion.

As for me and my trip, I had a wonderful time and saw so many magnificent sites, but yet I'm afraid I did exactly what I would advise others not to do: I spent so much time getting from one place to the next that I didn't have time to fully absorb the places I visited. A challenge in Iceland as it now stands is that because all the major sites are so spread apart, you spend all your time getting there. And then there's the weather to take into account. If your weather is miserable and you only have an hour somewhere, you could easily miss out on your best experience.

If, instead, you go somewhere and stay put for a few days, you then have the chance to do rainy-day things on rainy days, and nice-day things on nice days. I know some people like the idea of "doing" a country and considering it done, but in my opinion Iceland will be best enjoyed if you focus on one area per trip. Don't do the whole Ring Road in ten days like I did. It's too much, and you don't have time to appreciate what you're there to see.

You absolutely can have a perfectly nice trip if all you do is spend a long weekend doing the Golden Circle, Blue Lagoon, and a bit of downtown Reykjavík. I think, though, that the sweetness of Iceland, the beauty of Iceland, is best absorbed intimately. Savored. Iceland is a country for "slow tourism." You don't have to go to the top ten waterfalls to see a spectacular waterfall. My favorite waterfalls were those I "discovered" off the beaten path, little personal waterfalls that I had all to myself. No, they weren't like Dettifoss and Gullfoss, pouring kajillions of cubic feet of water per minute down to the depths below (I'm not sure if "kajillions of cubic feet of water per minute" is how the volume is measured, but I think it probably is), but they were still powerful and serene and beautiful.

I could totally imagine a group of friends, or a family, renting out a cottage or apartment or house, and using it as a base for a week or two. It would be a wonderful group vacation, and sharing accommodations and car rental, plus cooking for yourself in a place with a kitchen, makes an expensive country much more affordable. (Search on "self catering Iceland" and you'll find hundreds of options around the country. These often have a minimum three-night or even seven-night stay, but they are really affordable for groups. A warning: If you rent a place "off the beaten track," make sure you can get there in the car you rent. As I've noted many times, most 2WD cars are forbidden on some roads, including all "F" roads.

Make sure there are no forbidden roads on the way to your home away from home, or be sure to rent a car that can go there.)

But, back to my trip. I am never going to be able to not try to crunch everything I can into a trip. When I see that if I'm at X then I'm only a few miles from Y, I'll try to find a way to squeeze it in. Invariably, I'm exhausted. Driving sixteen hundred miles on this trip exacerbated that. I was dead tired at the end of every day, which left me little energy to go out and explore the towns at night. If I were to come back, I'd try to focus in on one area and soak in everything it has to offer. Having said that, I am glad to have had an overview of the whole country, because now I know what's out there. I'm never content to let someone else tell me what there is to see; I always have to see it myself. I guess I'll just have to find a way to travel more, so I can get back and see it all. Would I return to Iceland? Yes. I would avoid some of the "famous" sites, because many other sites in Iceland are just as spectacular but with fewer people. I would check out a few specialty day trips into places I can't go on my own, but I very much hope Iceland will work on infrastructure to make it easier to get into some of the interior. And if I went anytime other than summer, I'd be careful to thoroughly research what weather and road conditions I should expect. I would not want to drive many of those roads in snowy or icy weather. I drove the Ring Road in August and all was fine, but just a month later, in mid-September, people I know were trying to drive the same route, but found parts of the road were impassable due to weather — snow and ice.

Iceland is complex. Not too long ago it was all but cut off from the rest of the world. Now, it's a destination hot spot. There are growing pains. On top of this, the country and the people are dealing with an economic crash, and all signs point to the possibility that another is on the way. There are no easy answers. But what there is, is an extraordinarily gorgeous country full of interesting, warm, intelligent, people, and I have every confidence they will find their way through all these challenges, and come out of them better than ever.

On a final note, a fact that amused me: Filing away the brochures I gathered on the trip, I found a pamphlet that Car Rental Guy gave me on day one. On it is a map which shows the areas where passenger cars are not allowed to drive. The 862 between Ásbyrgi and Dettifoss, for example, is one of the roads passenger cars are not allowed on; you are, however, allowed on the paved portion from Dettifoss back to the Ring Road/Highway 1. The map also lists twelve roads "with high accident rate involving foreign drivers." I looked over the roads and realized I drove four of the twelve. Four! If only I'd looked at the map before taking off! The 864 — my only choice for the Diamond Circle — was among them, as was the 939, on the east coast, and the 59 and 54, which together make up the about 80 kilometers of gravel road I drove on my way to the Snæfellsnes peninsula. Having survived these roads, I feel like there should be some sort of T-shirt reward at the end. "I Survived the 939." Because I did.

Oh, and, for the record, my interview with Una was published the day after I got back. It was the most-read story at the site for several hours that day. Thank you, Una!

Now with all that said, a few thoughts on logistics, and some hindsight.

First, let's talk about money.

I have an ATM card that is NOT a debit card, that is, not attached to either Visa or Mastercard. Most banks have these available, but rarely will they offer them to you unless you ask. I got one because I believe if you use your debit card at a foreign ATM, and that debit card is attached to Visa or MC, I think you still incur the Visa/MC's foreign transaction fees. When I got my statements back, I saw that using the ATMs did incur the regular ATM fee (i.e., the, "This bank is going to charge you $2 to use this ATM, are you okay with that?" fee). However, as far as I can tell, I wasn't charged Visa/MC foreign transaction fees.

I could be wrong on all this, but that's how I think it works.

I used my credit cards for a lot of charges in part because it was hard to find ATMs, and in part because the money, being so different value-wise, was a little confusing to me. I had printed out a "cheat sheet" before I went, and had that tucked into my wallet, but I always feel pressure (probably self-induced) to finish transactions quickly. I probably need to learn to just slow down and take whatever time I need to take, to be sure I know what I'm doing.

I ended up with $72 in foreign transaction fees that I could have avoided if I'd used cash instead. (I'd still have had some bank fees, I think, but not $72 worth.)

This is the cheat sheet I used (at left), in case you want to make something like it for your own travels.

0.00826929	Exch. rate
ISK	USD
100	$0.83
200	$1.65
500	$4.13
1,000	$8.27
2,000	$16.54
5,000	$41.35
10,000	$82.69
20,000	$165.39
50,000	$413.46
100,000	$826.93
200,000	$1,653.86
500,000	$4,134.65
120.92983	Exch. rate
121	$1.00
242	$2.00
605	$5.00
1,209	$10.00
2,419	$20.00
6,046	$50.00
12,093	$100.00
24,186	$200.00
60,465	$500.00

Things I wish I'd done:

- Waterfall slow-motion video: My new camera can do slow-mo video. How cool would it have been to do slow-mo waterfall videos, and why did it not occur to me until after my trip, when I saw a video like that done by someone else? Would totally do this next time. Will do next time I'm near a waterfall.
- More video in general: As I said before, it is difficult to capture the vastness of Iceland, especially in pictures. Even panoramic photos don't do it, as the vastness is so vast. But the videos I took did capture some of that feel. More videos next time, to share with friends when I get home!

Items I packed, but didn't need:

- Waterproof sandals: I took a pair of waterproof (water tolerant) sandals because I wasn't sure whether the ground under the Blue Lagoon water would be rocky, or whether I'd need them walking from the changing room to the pool. As it turns out, the floor of the pools is not only smooth, it's slick, and I just walked barefoot from the changing room to the pools. If you're concerned about walking barefoot where others walk barefoot, then you might want flip flops. On the other hand, wash and dry your feet well and you should be fine, right?
- Tripod: I was going to video record my interviews, to use as publicity and to help my memory. This turned out to be unwieldy, though, and in one case wasn't allowed. And setting up a tripod to help with general pictures proved unneces-

sary, as I have an awesome camera with good image stabilization. At least I brought the light, compact tripod!

- Eye mask for night time: Yes, it was really light all night long. No, not all places I stayed had good blackout curtains. However, when I needed more darkness, I just draped a hand towel or piece of clothing over my face and called it good.

- Laundry detergent: It turned out that the place that had a laundromat, also had laundry detergent. Lesson: Check in advance to find out whether the laundromat you're using, or the hotel laundry, or whatever, provides laundry detergent.

- Hair dryer: As we know, my hair dryer blows Icelandic fuses. Lesson: Either ask in advance to ensure dryers at all places, or just buy a cheap dryer in the country you're going to. Blown fuses don't make for good mornings, believe me!

- Little tote bag: I had a day bag, which was all I needed. I brought along a collapsible tote bag — the kind that folds up to about the size of your palm — to carry groceries, etc., if I needed to, but I didn't need to. Note that in Iceland, as in some other countries, you have to bring your own bag for groceries. This one is not a 100 percent "wouldn't bring." If I had no day bag along, for sure I'd bring a tote bag. Good to have.

- Swim goggles: I have prescription swim goggles (not an exact prescription, just close enough) because I wear glasses and you generally don't want to swim in your glasses. However, as I learned, it's best not to get your hair wet at these pools. It wasn't until two days after my massage at Blue Lagoon, with the help of a lot of conditioner — a LOT — that I got my hair untangled. And my hair is very straight and generally doesn't tangle. My suggestion: Just keep your hair dry, to the extent you can. This means not actually swimming, which means I could just wear my regular glasses. (At one place, they did warn me that the soft grit in the water could scratch glasses, though, so just be careful.)

Items I packed, didn't use, but would still take:

- Rain jacket: Goes without saying in Iceland, or really almost any trip. I had good weather, but that wasn't guaranteed. As I was working on the above section, I got an email from my mom saying, "Look at Reykjavík weather forecast." Five days of heavy rain ahead. Five. Days. And it's still summer. The rain jacket I have is a thin shell, wraps up into a nice little packet, is easy to bring along and can be worn over almost anything, whether it's warm or cold.

- Camera manual: I got a new camera for this trip — an awesome new camera! But I didn't have time until just a few days before the trip to learn more about it. I don't think I used the manual, or I may have just used it once, but I'm glad I had it. A good picture is a terrible thing to miss!

- Copy of passport and credit cards, including emergency, out-of-country phone numbers for the credit cards (usually collect numbers): Again, goes without saying. Bring this along on every trip, but hopefully you'll never need it. Also, leave a copy with someone at home.

- Cell phone (the local one I purchased): Used once and was really glad to have it. I do wish it had a cover, because every time something would bump into it in my bag, the bleeping thing would beep (or "peep"). Still, I'll bring it again on every trip and just get a new SIM card.

- Conversion chart, ISK (Icelandic krona) to USD ($): I printed this up in advance to help me do quick conversions. I didn't look at it much but it was good to have, and took up hardly any space.

Items I packed, and am not sure I'd bring again:

- Umbrella: With the wind, the umbrella was almost useless. On the other hand, it's good to have in the case of a downpour, and the one I have is small.

Items I wish I'd brought:

- Swiss Army Knife with a bottle opener/corkscrew: I had one with a small knife, scissors, and nail file. Turns out the only thing I needed was a bottle opener and corkscrew.

Items I packed, and was really glad I packed:

- Shoes: I don't care what other people say about packing light; having at least two pairs so you can switch off is a good thing for your and others' noses. I did NOT bring along high heels, though, and felt no need to, despite the conversation my friend once overheard, where a Reykjavík local lamented the fact that tourists walk down the main shopping street dressed — horror of horrors! — in hiking boots. Having along a reasonably nice pair of shoes is fine, and locals can just deal with my lack of style.
- Picnic utensils: I have some sturdy, dishwasher-safe reusable plastic utensils that I bought just for travel. I take them on every trip and always have a use for them. If you're trying to save money by not eating in restaurants, it's so handy to have your own spoon for your Skyr yogurt, or a fork for the salad you buy at the deli.

- Power adapters: I brought three, one specific to my laptop, plus two others. This way I was able to recharge both my iPhone and my Icelandic phone, or have my camera battery recharger going while I charged my phone, and so on. Two was enough; three would have been handy sometimes, but I'm not sure I always had enough plugs to handle all the power adapters anyway. Two plus the laptop adapter seemed to be a good number.

A Note About Credibility

I had no idea when I started writing these books that I'd need to write this disclaimer. In case anyone wonders, the ideas in the Pam on the Map books, all opinions and accounts, are purely my own. They have not been bought by any company. I never will agree to give a positive review or account in exchange for a free anything. I didn't expect to face that dilemma so early in my travel writing, but one day I found myself being offered a free experience if, in exchange, I promised not to say anything negative about the company in public. I declined. My honesty, my personal integrity, and my credibility with readers are far too important to me. Will I accept free trips and offers? Sure! Absolutely! Bring it on! I love free stuff! But never will I do so if the offer hinges on agreeing to mislead readers.

In today's travel world, many bloggers and other writers are getting free trips, free products, free everything, and from the fact that the reviews are almost always glowing, I'm assuming that positive report is part of the deal. I disagree with this philosophy. I think it only hurts companies in the end if consumers learn they can't trust them. Whatever the relationship — company/consumer, friend/friend, author/reader, anything — trust and honesty have to be at the core for that relationship to thrive. I firmly believe this. And, therefore, you can be sure that the opinions in these books (and anywhere you find me) have never been and will never be bought or owned by anyone but me.

Photos and Reviews

Photos

I debated adding photos to these books, but in the end decided not to due to issues of cost and quality control. But fear not, photo-loving people! I've put a bunch of pictures up on my website. Just go to www.pamstucky.com/pamonthemap/iceland and peruse some Iceland photos to your heart's content!

Reviews

Word-of-mouth and reader reviews are my best marketing. If you enjoyed this book, I would be so grateful if you would tell your friends and/or write a quick review! And be sure to find me online and say hello! Thank you!

Acknowledgments

In some ways, I want to thank everyone in Iceland. It's such a small country, and as I said, it feels like everyone is connected. Iceland's population feels so intimate. Therefore, people of Iceland, I thank you all. Thank you for sharing your country with me, for your warmth and openness and thoughtfulness. I was delighted to spend some time in your wonderful home.

My two favorite Icelandic authors, Yrsa Sigurðardóttir and Ragnar Jónasson, thank you so much for your time. Yrsa, I still have your book and plan to open it on some very bright day when I am surrounded by people who will protect me from the frights inside! I wish you all the best with your movie. Ragnar, I hope your books are translated into English soon so I can enjoy them, too! And I hope your TV series is everything you wish for. With the two of you at the helm, I am sure Iceland Noir will exceed all expectations and be a brilliant success.

Ragnar Þorvarðarson, thank you so much for answering my random email, and for taking me along for the ice cream car ride.

I thoroughly enjoyed our conversation; it was one of the highlights of my trip. I hope your new endeavors bring you every joy.

Thank you to Unnur Margrét Arnardóttir for kindly working with me to arrange my meeting with Jón Gnarr, and thank you to Jón Gnarr for an interview that will always be one of my favorites; meeting you was a delight. Shortly after this book comes out, the world will find out whether you've decided to run for another term as mayor. Wherever life takes you, I hope you are always able to approach it with the happiness and joy for life you shared with me.

Thank you so much to Eiríkur Björn Björgvinsson for going out of your way to meet up with me in a time of great stress and sorrow; your passion and pride in your people and city were wonderful to witness. Next time I come to Akureyri, I hope you'll point the way for me to those lights on the side of the mountain, the Heart of the North!

To all the other individuals who shared their time and tales with me, so many thanks. In some cases I know your names but am leaving them out for privacy's sake, and in some cases, I don't know your names, for which I apologize. I am nevertheless so grateful for all your thoughts and insights and kindness: Sif Svavarsdóttir, Café Girl, Car Rental Guy, Front Desk Guy, Visitor Centre Guy and Gal, and all the rest. And Una Sighvatsdóttir, thank you for interviewing me and making me feel the slightest bit famous for a day!

Kay Schrag, thank you for helping me figure out my camera just before I left on my trip, so I had a slightly better chance of getting slightly better pictures.

Tremendous, enormous, gigantic thanks to Mary Frances Davidson and her family, for putting me up and putting up with me. (Special thanks to Mary Frances's son, with my apologies for having taken his room from him for a few nights.) I am so grateful for the hospitality, and I'm especially grateful for all the insights and wisdom and thoughts you shared with me about Iceland, Icelanders, and the world. This trip would not have been nearly as wonderful without you!

Supporters and fans and friends online, your encouragement means the world to me. Writing is a vulnerable career, and you are always there to support and inspire me and cheer me on. When I'm feeling discouraged or low, I can always count on you to remind me why I love to write. Thank you.

I know I've said this before, but truly, I am amazed by how supportive all the people in my life are, how much they believe in me. It even brings me to tears, sometimes, how amazing these people are. Friends and family with unwavering belief in me, who would do anything they could to help me. You know who you are, and don't think I don't notice. I can't even put into words how grateful I am.

Donna Hostick, thank you for sharing with me your insights from your own trip to Iceland, to help me better tell the tale of my own, and for your never-ending support and advocacy of me and my writing. It means so much. Of all my sisters, you will always be my favorite.

Mom and Dad, what can I say? Of all the parents in the world, and I got the very best two. My gratitude knows no bounds for all you do and are.

Thank you, everyone!

Praise for Pam Stucky's Wishing Rock series

"We are very proud to announce that *Letters From Wishing Rock* by Pam Stucky is a 2013 B.R.A.G. Medallion Honoree. This signifies that this book is well worth a reader's time and money!"

— *Indie B.R.A.G.,*
www.bragmedallion.com

Letters from Wishing Rock has been awarded the Awesome Indies Seal of Approval

— *www.awesomeindies.net*

"Just what the doctor ordered, fresh, quirky, funny in places and seasoned with wisdom. Light without being frivolous, it follows the story of a woman trying to find someone to fill her desire for true love and family. The inhabitants of Wishing Rock embody this sense of family in the most delightful way, and I fell in love with the characters in a flash, especially Gran. The rhythm the author created with the different length emails and occasional texts was skillfully done and gave an almost musical undercurrent to the text. The characters are delightful and the recipes a nice touch. The travels in Scotland made me want to visit." (referring to *Letters from Wishing Rock*)

— *Tahlia Newland, author of* Lethal Inheritance

"This was a book I stayed up late to read, because reading it felt like sitting comfortably by the fire, talking with my nicest and funniest friends, all of whom had uplifting and sometimes hilarious thoughts to share. As the story progressed, not only did I become more curious about how all the characters' adventures would turn out, but I found myself thinking along the same philosophical lines as they were, regarding how to make one's life happier. Her writing, in the voices of the various characters, is witty and wise, and I found myself grinning or giggling at several of the observations."

— *Molly Ringle, author of* What Scotland Taught Me

"I wish this series would have been around when I was younger and still trying to figure out what I wanted in a relationship and in life in general. So many wise words, and more than once I went back and reread a page or two because it struck such a chord with me."

— *PLL, Amazon reviewer*

"Ms. Stucky's novels are fantastic! A fresh approach to writing that takes readers into the lives of the characters (which are all interesting and fun). I never wanted the books to end! The concepts of happiness, joy, and love are all addressed in ways that are thought-provoking and so much fun to read. I love the fact that the characters are so real, and the story is so believable. I recommend this book to anyone, but especially someone that you think might benefit from a new way of looking at happiness in life. Thank you Ms. Stucky! "

— *SJ, Amazon reviewer*

Letters from Wishing Rock (a novel with recipes)
The Wishing Rock Theory of Life (a novel with recipes)
The Tides of Wishing Rock (a novel with recipes)